Does Immigration Increase Crime?

Do migrants lead to an increase in crime rates in their host societies? This highly contentious issue has become a mainstay in the political debate and a lightning rod for the galvanization of populist movements, despite often lacking any empirical support. In this game-changing book, the authors examine what the existing data actually says, and provide their own novel evidence on the immigration-crime connection. Taking the unusual approach of analysing the subject from an economic perspective, the authors build on the pioneering work of Nobel Prize winner Gary Becker to construct their innovative arguments. By considering evidence from different countries, with a focus on establishing causal relationships, the authors are able to analyse not only if migrants do cause crime but also whether migration policies can play a role in shaping incentives for migrants to engage in crime. This book will appeal to students and academics across the social sciences, as well as citizens interested in this topical issue.

FRANCESCO FASANI is Associate Professor in Economics at Queen Mary University of London. He is a Research Affiliate at CEPR (Centre for Economic Policy Research) and a Research Fellow at CReAM (Centre for Research and Analysis of Migration) and IZA (Institute for the Study of Labor, Bonn).

GIOVANNI MASTROBUONI is Carlo Alberto Chair at the Collegio Carlo Alberto and Professor in Economics at the University of Turin, ESOMAS, and at the University of Essex. He is a research fellow at the Institute for the Study of Labor in Bonn and editor of the The B.E. Journal of Economic Analysis and Policy.

EMILY G. OWENS is Professor of Criminology, Law and Society, and Economics at the University of California, Irvine. She is an associate editor of the Journal of Quantitative Criminology, a senior research fellow at the Police Foundation, and a fellow of the Academy of Experimental Criminology.

PAOLO PINOTTI is Endowed Associate Professor in Economic Analysis of Crime at the Department of Social and Political Sciences at Bocconi University. His other roles include Coordinator of Fondazione Rodolfo Debenedetti, Director of the CLEAN Unit on the economics of crime at the Baffi-Carefin Center, Senior Researcher at FBK-Irvapp.

Does Immigration Increase Crime?

Migration Policy and the Creation of the Criminal Immigrant

FRANCESCO FASANI
Queen Mary University of London

GIOVANNI MASTROBUONI
Collegio Carlo Alberto, University of Turin and University of Essex

EMILY G. OWENS
University of California, Irvine

PAOLO PINOTTI
Bocconi University and Fondazione Rodolfo Debenedetti

CAMBRIDGE
UNIVERSITY PRESS

CAMBRIDGE
UNIVERSITY PRESS

University Printing House, Cambridge CB2 8BS, United Kingdom

One Liberty Plaza, 20th Floor, New York, NY 10006, USA

477 Williamstown Road, Port Melbourne, VIC 3207, Australia

314–321, 3rd Floor, Plot 3, Splendor Forum, Jasola District Centre,
New Delhi – 110025, India

79 Anson Road, #06–04/06, Singapore 079906

Cambridge University Press is part of the University of Cambridge.

It furthers the University's mission by disseminating knowledge in the pursuit of
education, learning, and research at the highest international levels of excellence.

www.cambridge.org
Information on this title: www.cambridge.org/9781108494557
DOI: 10.1017/9781108626286

© Francesco Fasani, Giovanni Mastrobuoni, Emily Owens, and Paolo Pinotti 2019

First published 2019

Printed in the United Kingdom by TJ International Ltd, Padstow Cornwall

A catalogue record for this publication is available from the British Library.

ISBN 978-1-108-49455-7 Hardback
ISBN 978-1-108-73177-5 Paperback

Contents

Figures

Tables

Acknowledgements

This research was possible thanks to generous funding from Fondazione Rodolfo Debenedetti. We thank the Italian Ministry of Interior for disclosing the data on residence permits and crime; Giancarlo Blangiardo (ISMU) for providing part of the data used in Chapter 2; and Josh Angrist, Randi Hjalmarsson, Stephen Machin, Nicola Persico, and Luigi Pistaferri for invaluable comments on an earlier draft of this work. We also thank Dimitrios Bermperoglou, Giammarco Cezza, Chiara Serra, Giulia Tagliaferri, and Giulia Tomaselli for excellent research assistance.

Introduction

International flows of people are a distinctive trait of our contemporary globalized world, as much as are international flows of goods, services, and ideas. Differently from the latter, however, migration faces a fierce opposition in most destination countries (Hatton and Williamson, 2005; Mayda, 2008). One reason for this may be that natives and immigrants compete for the same jobs and welfare programs. Indeed, foreign immigrants are sometimes blamed for hurting the labour market prospects of native workers – particularly the low-skilled ones – and for imposing an additional burden on welfare expenditure (Scheve and Slaughter, 2001; Mayda, 2006; Hanson et al., 2007; Facchini and Mayda, 2009; Ortega and Polavieja, 2012). In most countries, however, natives are far more concerned that immigrants increase crime, rather than unemployment or taxes. Indeed, fears of immigrants' involvement in crime are at the center of the public and political debate about immigration and have been a major reason for the rise of anti-immigrant parties in several European countries (Dinas and van Spanje, 2011).

Partly in response to such concerns, a large academic literature has examined the relationship between immigration and crime. Many researchers, most notably Sampson (2008), argue that there is, in fact, a US 'Latino Paradox', in that first-generation immigrants to the USA from Mexico appear to engage in crime at much lower rates than would be predicted based on their socio-economic status. Others, such as Shihadeh and Barranco (2010, 2013), argue that more recent waves of migrants from other parts of Latin America are less likely to be associated with crime reductions, and may even increase the crime rates of natives. Recently, Ousey and Kubrin (2018) conducted a review of more than 500 papers published between 1994 and 2014 in sociology, criminology, and political science that analysed the relationship between immigration and crime. In sharp contrast to public perception, Ousey and Kubrin conclude that higher rates of immigration are likely associated with slightly reduced rates of crime.

Butcher and Piehl (1998) provide the first systematic economic analysis of immigration and crime rates, showing that immigration did not lead to a significant increase in crime across US cities over the period 1980–90. Reid et al. (2005) and Wadsworth (2010) reached the same conclusion when looking at more recent periods. Moving to European countries, Bianchi et al. (2012) concluded that immigration did not increased crime across Italian provinces, while Alonso-Borrego et al. (2012) estimated a positive relationship between immigration and crime in Spain. Finally, Bell et al. (2013) focused on two large waves of recent UK immigration, namely the late 1990s/early 2000s asylum seekers and the post-2004 inflow from EU accession countries, respectively. They found that only in the former case was there a significant increase in (property) crimes.

This last result suggests that the propensity to engage in crime may vary strongly with social context and the composition of the immigrant population. Indeed, this is consistent with the choice-theoretic model of crime (Becker, 1968), which posits that individuals choose whether to engage in crime or not by comparing the relative costs and benefits of legitimate and illegitimate activities. The latter generally depend on several individual characteristics such as age, gender, education, etc., all of which could vary across different groups of immigrants just as they vary across other groups of people. However, immigrants differ among themselves along an additional, crucial dimension: legal status in their destination country. The focus of this book is to systematically explore how government policies that affect the legal status of immigrants influence the immigrant–crime relationship. From a practical perspective, politicians and policy-makers have, at best, only limited control over how many immigrants are in their country at a given time. What is under government control, however, are the policies in place that affect how those immigrants will interact with society.

Legal status may profoundly affect criminal behaviour by changing the relative payoffs of legitimate and illegitimate activities. In most destination countries, legal status is a prerequisite for working in the official economy. Therefore, undocumented immigrants are excluded from legitimate economic activities or they may be able to work just in the shadow economy. In either case, they would face worse (legitimate) income opportunities compared to legal immigrants and thus a lower opportunity cost of crime.

In spite of the importance of the relationship between immigration police and crime for the debate on immigration reforms currently taking place in the USA as well as in many European countries, there is very little empirical evidence on this topic. One important reason is that it is generally very difficult to observe undocumented immigrants, not to mention their involvement in criminal activity.

In this book we address these issues for three main destination countries: Italy, the UK, and the USA. Chapter 1 motivates the analysis by presenting recent survey evidence on natives' attitudes toward immigrants in a number of countries in North America and Europe, as well as some stylized facts about immigrants' involvement in crime. In the majority of countries, natives are mostly concerned that immigrants – particularly the undocumented – increase crime rates, as opposed to unemployment or taxes. When moving from perceptions to criminal statistics, immigrants are over-represented among offenders in most, but not all, Organisation for Economic Co-operation and Development (OECD) countries. At the same time, the surge in immigration was *not* accompanied by an increase in crime rates over time and across countries. We discuss a potential explanation for this apparent puzzle as well as the limitations of cross-country estimates. In particular, average estimates across countries may mask a significant heterogeneity in the effect of different groups of immigrants, notably between documented and undocumented immigrants.

These two groups differ mainly along two dimensions. First, undocumented immigrants cannot work in the official economy, thus facing worse employment and income opportunities. Second, they can be expelled and deported back to their home country. These provisions have important (and ambiguous) implications for the number of crimes committed in destination countries. On the one hand, undocumented immigrants who are not deported face a lower opportunity cost – and, thus, a higher probability of – committing crimes. On the other hand, undocumented immigrants who are actually deported would no longer commit crimes in the destination country, which mechanically reduces the crime rate of this group. From a theoretical perspective, the effect of legal status is thus ambiguous.

The main threat to estimating such effect is that, typically, legal and undocumented immigrants differ with respect to many other characteristics (in addition to legal status). In particular, the former group may have a lower probability of engaging in crime to start with – independently of the effect of legal status. Therefore, selection into legal status may bias the estimates towards finding a negative effect of legal status on crime.

An attempt to overcome these identification difficulties is proposed by Mastrobuoni and Pinotti (2015), who exploit a large-scale amnesty of prison inmates in Italy (in August 2006) and the last round of the EU enlargement (five months later, in January 2007) as a natural experiment to separately identify causality from selection. They show that the recidivism of citizens from newly admitted EU countries, who obtained legal status in all EU member countries (including Italy), decreased from 5.8 to 2.3 percentage points over a six-month period after the EU accession, as compared to no change in a control group of inmates from EU candidate member countries. This result suggests that access to legal status significantly reduced the propensity to engage in criminal behaviour, and that such effect prevailed over the potential increase in crime caused by the stop of deportations. However, it is unclear whether this conclusion can be generalized to the entire immigrant population (as opposed to former prison inmates) and to differences in legal status that are routinely induced by migration policy (as opposed to one-off changes induced by the EU enlargement).

To answer these questions, in Chapter 2 we investigate the effect of changes in legal status induced by the current migration policy in Italy. In recent years, Italian migration policy has been based on a system of migration quotas by country of origin, type of permit, and province of destination. Such institutional framework is by no means specific to the Italian context, as analogous quota-based policies are currently adopted in many destination countries (e.g. Austria, Canada, and Spain). One peculiarity of the Italian system lies in the tight rationing of permits, as total quotas are always substantially lower than the number of applications for residence permits. Moreover, it is well understood that, in the Italian context, the quota system is used mainly to legalize undocumented workers already resident in the country rather than to regulate entries of new workers. These facts, in addition to a low enforcement of migration restrictions, have led to the formation of large pools of unauthorized entrants and to the recurrent need for generalized amnesties of illegal immigrants.

We exploit these features of Italian migration policy to estimate the effect of legal status on crime across Italian regions and provinces. We first take advantage of the electronic procedure to apply for residence permits, introduced in year 2007, to estimate the effect of legal status at the individual level. Starting in that year, applications must be sent electronically during given 'click days' of the year, and they are processed on a first-come, first-served basis until depletion of available quotas. Matching the administrative records of applicants with individual police files, we find that individuals whose applications are received just after the depletion of quotas (and are thus denied legal status) commit more serious crimes during the year after the amnesty compared to individuals whose applications are received just before the cutoff.

We then estimate the relationship between changes in crime and the share of applicants obtaining legal status with the last four general amnesties (1991, 1995, 1998, and 2002). This analysis suggests that, in the year following an amnesty, regions in which a higher share of immigrants obtained legal status experience a greater decline in immigrant crime rates, relative to the other regions.

Overall, our findings suggest that access to legal status reduces the number of crimes committed by immigrants in Italy. Nevertheless, policies that grant legal status to undocumented workers who are already residing in the country can only be considered second-best policy interventions. Indeed, their short-term beneficial effect on crime may be completely offset by the expectation that similar policies will be implemented again in the future, which incentivises inflows of undocumented immigrants. Rather than ex post legalization of unauthorized immigrants, Italy could steer its migration policy towards creating better possibilities and incentives for legal entry into and legal participation in its labour market.

The limitations of Italian migration policy probably reflect, among other things, its limited experience as an immigration country. In Chapters 3 and 4, we focus respectively on the UK and the USA, which have a long tradition of immigration.

The UK is a major recipient of migrant inflows from both other European countries and the rest of the world. The UK started receiving large cohorts of foreign born workers in the 1960s–70s, and its immigrant population has grown considerably in recent years, particularly after the EU enlargements in 2004 and 2007. These sudden changes provide researchers with a very interesting setting in which to explore the immigration–crime link. In Chapter 3, we start by documenting recent developments in the British immigration policy, trends in numbers and flows of its immigrant population, and migrants' main nationalities and educational levels. We then describe recent changes in offending rate in the UK, distinguishing among different types of crimes and focusing on the evidence of immigrant involvement in criminal activities in the UK. As we discuss in the chapter, in spite of an immigrant population that almost doubled in the last fifteen years, the crime rate kept declining over the same period of time.

After having discussed all this descriptive evidence, we address the following empirical question: Has the arrival of novel and large immigrant waves made the UK a more dangerous country in recent years? We answer this question by comparing aggregate trends in immigrant population and crime, by discussing judicial statistics, and by developing a novel econometric analysis of the impact of immigration on local crime rates. Far from uncovering a clear increase in local crime due to a higher presence for immigrants in the area, we generally find no significant effect, and some estimates point in the opposite direction, suggesting that immigrants on average are associated with lower crime rates. In further results, we investigate whether the relationship between crime and immigration residents has changed in response to the Great Recession. We find evidence consistent with a standard economic model of crime, whereby more offending is observed when economic conditions worsen.

In Chapter 4, we turn to the USA, where immigration and crime control are, for the most part, functions of different government bodies; immigration is regulated by the federal government, whereas most crime control is done by states. Despite this administrative separation, we document the extent to which immigration policy has historically reflected concerns about the criminal behaviour of potential immigrants, and has been designed to explicitly address fear of criminal aliens. We pay special attention to one of the larger historic shifts in immigration police, the 1917 Literacy Act, which made literacy a requirement for adult men hoping to move to the USA. Using Census data on immigration dates, literacy, and incarceration status, we show that the enactment of the literacy test changed the composition of immigrants in a way that both increased human capital and also lowered the incarceration rate of immigrants. The combination of these two effects confirms the Italian experience of immigration and crime; in the same way that native residents with low levels of human capital are more likely to engage in crime, immigrants with skills that are rewarded in the legal labour market, in this case, reading ability, are less likely to offend. Finally, we also discuss new research assessing the impact of the 1986 Immigration Reform and Control Act (IRCA), a Reagan–era bill that conferred 'amnesty' on undocumented immigrants currently in the USA while attempting to limit the flow of future undocumented migrants into the country. Without taking a stand on the impact of IRCA on the flow of immigrants, our focus here is on the impact of policies that affected the ability of those immigrants to assimilate into US society, in particular the conferral of official 'legal status' and the restrictions on employing undocumented workers.

Finally, we discuss more recent research that takes a 'sending country' rather than 'receiving country' focus. Refugees from conflict-prone areas are entering developed countries in ever greater numbers. Whether our previous results generalize to these immigrants is our final research question. In Chapter 5, we examine the experience of countries in the EU, where the number of refugees almost doubled from 2014 to 2016, reaching 1.8 million. In spite of active and vocal public concern, we find no evidence of a link between refugees and crime.

This book is structured as follows. In Chapter 1, we report some evidence on perceptions about immigration and the involvement of immigrants in crime across several OECD countries, and we discuss the relationship between immigrant legal status and criminal behaviour. Then Chapters 2, 3, and 4 empirically investigate such relationship in Italy, the UK, and the USA, respectively. Chapter 5 takes a cross-country perspective to investigate the relationship between refugees and crime. Finally, we conclude with some remarks on what we learned.

I Immigration and Crime: Perceptions and Reality

Immigration is a contentious issue in most destination countries. From a purely economic perspective, the removal of barriers to labour mobility would allow for the efficient allocation of productive factors at the global level. At the same time, its distributional consequences may undermine the political support for the free movement of people across countries. Most importantly, natives in destination countries may oppose immigration on grounds other than just labour market competition. Indeed, natives in destination countries are mostly concerned that immigration increases crime.

In this chapter, we document this conclusion using data from a large, multi-country opinion survey. Importantly, the results of the survey suggest that natives tend to overstate the size of the immigrant population and that opposition to immigration is driven to a significant extent by such misperceptions. For this reason, in the second part of the chapter we confront such concerns with statistics on long-run trends in immigration and crime across Organisation for Economic Co-operation and Development (OECD) countries.

I.I ATTITUDES TOWARDS MIGRANTS

Transatlantic Trends is an authoritative survey on a wide range of economic and political issues. It has been conducted annually between 2002 and 2011 in a number of North American and European countries. Starting in 2008, the survey included an ad hoc module on immigration, covering issues such as the integration of immigrants, their impacts on the labour market of the host countries, and preferences about migration policy.[1] Although the

---
[1] The survey is a joint project of the German Marshall Fund of the United States, the Compagnia di San Paolo, and the Barrow Cadbury Trust, with additional support from

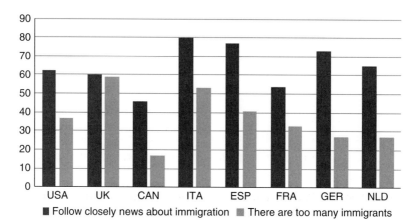

FIGURE I.I Natives' concerns about immigration.

Note: The graph shows measures of attitudes towards migration in a number of North American and European countries, based on the results of the TTS (http://trends.gmfus.org/immigration/about/).

sample of countries is smaller than in other multi-country surveys (e.g. the World Values Survey, the International Social Survey Programs, or the European Social Survey), its specific focus on migration issues allows for a much deeper understanding of attitudes towards this phenomenon.[2]

The first important element that emerges from the survey is the salience of immigration in the public debate. Indeed, the majority of respondents in each country follow closely news about immigration. Most importantly, a very large share of people in all countries believe that the number of immigrants is excessively high (see Figure 1.1), especially in Anglo-Saxon countries (with the notable exception of Canada) and in Southern Europe. In particular, those calling for a reduction in the presence of foreigners represent the majority of respondents in the UK and Italy. Anti-immigrant sentiments are less

the Fundación BBVA. The number of people interviewed in each country is around 1,000. Additional information is available through http://trends.gmfus.org/immigration/about/

2   The USA, UK, Italy, Germany, the Netherlands, and France were included in all waves of the Transatlantic Trends Survey (TTS) since 2008; Canada and Spain were included after 2010.

widespread in the rest of continental Europe (France, Germany, and the Netherlands), where opponents to migration account for one-fourth to one-third of the respondents.

Another measure of opposition to migration, and one that is very relevant for the political economy of migration restrictions, is the electoral support for parties that have an explicit anti-immigrant stance. Figure 1.2 plots the share of votes obtained by some of these parties at the elections for the European Parliament in 2004, 2009, and 2014, respectively. The National Front, UK Independence Party, and Danish People's Party reached 25% of the votes at the 2014 elections. Other anti-immigrant parties, such as the Freedom Party in Austria and the Northern League in Italy, are key players in the formation of national governments. Outside Europe, Donald Trump won the 2016 US presidential election running on a markedly anti-immigrant platform that featured, among other issues, the deportation of undocumented immigrants and the 'Mexico Wall'.

Regarding the main reasons for opposition to migration, the economics literature has traditionally focused on competition between immigrants and natives in labour markets and in the use of social services. Starting with the former dimension, if foreign and native workers are perfectly substitutable in production and the demand for labour is downward sloping, immigrants would exert a downward pressure on wages. However, the elasticity of substitution between foreign and native workers may be less than infinite, or even lower than unity – meaning that the two groups of workers are complements in production. In practice, there is no empirical consensus as to the effect of immigration on natives' wages and employment in the USA or other destination countries.[3]

---

[3] For the USA, Borjas (2003) estimates a 0.3 to 0.4 elasticity of natives' wages to labour supply shifts across education–experience cells. By contrast, Card (2001) concludes that immigration had no negative effect on natives' wages across geographical areas, and Ottaviano and Peri (2012) go as far as suggesting complementarity between immigrants and natives. Turning to the case of the UK, Dustmann et al. (2012) show that immigration depresses wages below the 20th percentile of the wage distribution, while it benefits natives at the top of the wage distribution. Kerr and Kerr (2011) provide a survey of this literature.

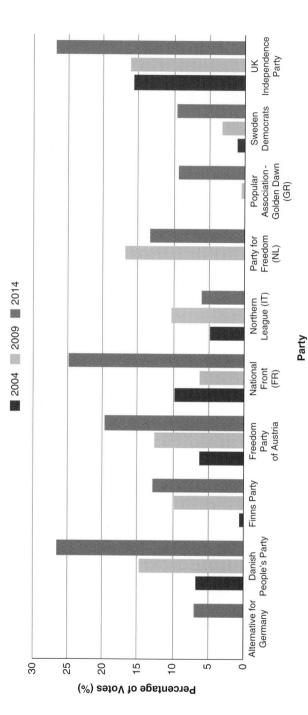

FIGURE I.2 Percentage vote share of some anti-immigrant parties at European Parliament elections, 2004–14.

Note: The graph shows the share of votes obtained by some anti-immigrant parties at European Parliament elections in 2004, 2009, and 2014.

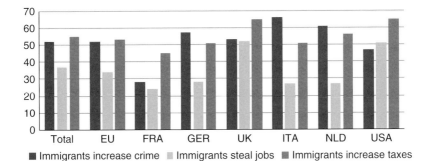

FIGURE I.3 Concerns about the impact of immigrants on jobs, taxes, and crime rates.

Note: The graph shows the fraction of people worried that immigrants increase unemployment, taxes, and crime rates, based on the results of the TTS (http://trends.gmfus.org/immigration/about/).

Turning to competition for social services, the effect is also unclear. On the one hand, immigrants have generally lower incomes and higher fertility rates than natives, which implies greater dependence on government expenditures for services such as education, emergency health services, and some income-transfer programs. On the other hand, immigrants also tend to be younger and exhibit higher employment rates than natives, and young workers contribute disproportionately to total payroll tax collections. Therefore, the net effect of immigration on government receipts and expenditures depends crucially on the age and skill distribution of immigrants relative to that of natives (Storesletten, 2000).

Overall, the evidence on the effects of immigration on labour market outcomes and provision of social services remains mixed. Nevertheless, both issues are important determinants of opposition to migration. In particular, the 2008 wave of the TTS asks whether 'immigrants take jobs away from the native born' and 'immigration in general will cause taxes to be raised because of immigrants' demand for social services'. Figure 1.3 shows that the latter concern is prevalent in all countries, while fears over the labour market impacts of immigration are much more widespread in the UK and the USA.

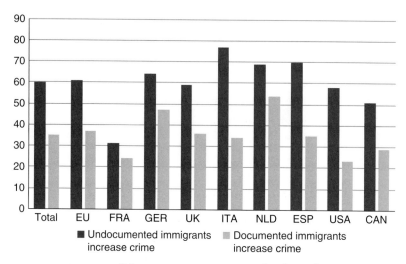

FIGURE 1.4 Crime rate concerns associated with regular and irregular immigrants.

Note: The graph shows the fraction of TTS respondents worried that regular and irregular immigrants increase crime rates.

Interestingly, such countries are characterized by flexible labour markets, in which natives may be more exposed to competition from immigrants.[4]

The most striking result that emerges from Figure 1.3, however, is that a very large share of people in all countries are afraid of immigration for reasons unrelated to labour market conditions, believing "Immigration in general will increase crime in our society." The majority of people in the UK, Germany, Italy, and the Netherlands believe that this is actually the case, and in the latter three countries there are more people concerned about crime effects than about anything else.

Therefore, political demand for migration restrictions may be driven largely by fears that immigration increases crime, rather than by concerns about personal or government income. At the same time,

---

[4] For an extensive analysis of the empirical relationship between exposure to labour market competition and natives' attitudes towards migrants see Facchini and Mayda (2008, 2009).

crime concerns are not directed towards all immigrants in the same way. In the 2009 wave of the survey, respondents were allowed to distinguish between 'regular' (fully documented) and 'irregular' (undocumented) immigrants. Most respondents maintained a clear distinction between the two groups: while the irregulars are generally blamed for increasing crime, regular immigrants cause much less concern in all countries (see Figure 1.4).

1.2 REGULAR AND IRREGULAR MIGRATION: PERCEPTIONS AND REALITY

The evidence just discussed confirms that crime concerns – particularly towards illegal immigrants – are an important component of natives' attitudes towards immigrants. At the same time, natives' concerns (as measured by opinion surveys or by electoral support for xenophobic parties) may not be very informative about the actual effect of immigration on crime rates, because people may have biased beliefs about both phenomena.

These biases are indeed apparent also in the 2010 wave of the TTS. In that year, respondents in each country were randomly split into two groups: those in the first group were simply asked whether they believed that there are 'too many immigrants', whereas respondents in the second group were asked the same question after being informed of the actual presence of (regular) immigrants compared with total residents. According to the OECD Migration Statistics, for the countries included in the TTS, such a share ranges between 5% and 13% (see Figure 1.5).

Figure 1.6 shows that access to this information by a (randomly chosen) group of respondents dramatically lowers their concerns about excessive immigration. This simple test suggests that opposition to migration may reflect, at least in part, a general tendency to overestimate the number of immigrants who are actually present in the country.

Cognitive biases seem even more pronounced for irregular migration, which is undoubtedly harder to quantify; still, estimates

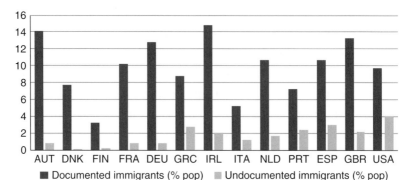

FIGURE 1.5 Share of regular and irregular immigrants over the total resident population.

Note: The graph shows the average share of regular and irregular immigrants over the total resident population in a number of countries during the period 2002–08. The data on regular immigrants come from the OECD Population Statistics, while the sources of data for irregular immigrants in Europe and the USA are the Clandestino Project (http://clandestino.eliamep.gr/) and the US Department of Homeland Security (Hoefer et al., 2009), respectively.

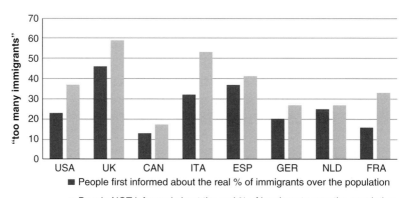

FIGURE 1.6 Information and concerns about excessive immigration.

Note: The graph compares the fraction of people worried about excessive immigration between two random subsamples of the TTS in each country. The grey bars refer to subsamples of individuals who were previously informed about the true fraction of foreigners in the population, while the black bars refer to subsamples of people who did not receive such information.

of this phenomenon can be obtained using a variety of methods. For instance, generalized amnesties of irregular immigrants allow counting applications sent by foreigners who are unofficially present in the country. This method has been employed often in Italy, where several amnesties have been conducted since the mid-1980s. Alternatively, one may compare the (cumulative) number of residence and/or working permits issued during a given period with the total number of foreigners, as reported in the national census. This second method was used, for instance, by Hoefer et al. (2009).

Figure 1.5 shows a collection of estimates of the number of undocumented immigrants in different receiving countries around 2005, as provided by the Clandestino Project.[5] In all countries, the share of undocumented immigrants over total foreigners remains relatively small – between less than one-tenth in France and Germany to about one-third in the USA. However, the majority of respondents in Italy, the USA, and Spain (65%, 58%, and 50%, respectively), as well as a sizeable fraction of the respondents in other countries (from 11% in Germany to 38% in the UK), believe that the majority of immigrants are present in the country irregularly.

This tendency to overestimate the number of irregular immigrants may partly explain concerns about immigration. Similarly, natives may have biased perceptions about immigrants' involvement in crime. For these reasons, we next move from perceptions to official statistics on immigration and crime.

1.3 EVIDENCE FROM INCARCERATION RATES

Against the backdrop of an increasing integration of the world economy, international migration has also been growing at a fast pace since

---

[5] The Clandestino Project was financed within the sixth EU framework and provides upper and lower bound estimates for the size of the irregular immigrant population in several European countries in three benchmark years (2002, 2005, and 2008). The documentation and the data are publicly available through the website http://clandes tino.eliamep.gr/. As the project does not cover countries outside Europe, we took the estimate of the undocumented population in the USA from the Department of Homeland Security (Hoefer et al., 2009).

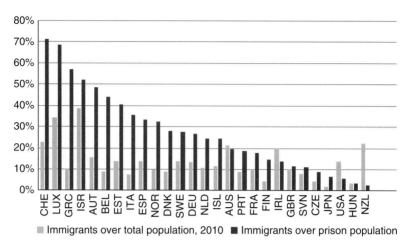

FIGURE 1.7 Immigrants' incarceration rates across countries.
Note: The graph shows the fraction of foreigners in the total resident population (light bars) and in the prison population (dark bars).
Source: OECD and Centre for Prison Studies (www.prisonstudies.org/).

the early 1980s. Between 1980 and 2010, the number of foreign immigrants in OECD countries more than doubled, from 38 to 87 million (6.5% to 12% of the total resident population, respectively).

In most of these countries, immigrants represent an even larger fraction of the prison population (see Figure 1.7). Although the incarceration rate is a very crude measure of involvement in criminal activity, it is the only one available separately for immigrants and natives in a large sample of countries.[6] In the same graph, we also report the share of foreigners over the total population during the same period, including both regular and (the estimated number of) irregular immigrants. In the greatest majority of destination countries – especially in continental Europe – immigrants are greatly over-represented among criminal offenders. For instance, in 2010 immigrants in Italy represented 35.6% of the prison population but just 7.4% of residents. By contrast, immigrants in the USA have a lower probability of being incarcerated compared to natives. A potential explanation for this fact

---

[6]   The source of data on incarceration is the International Centre for Prison Studies (www .prisonstudies.org/). The data always refer to the most recent available year.

is that the flexible labour market in the USA offers more employment opportunities to immigrants than do most EU countries, which theoretically could lower their propensity to engage in crime while at the same time increasing competition between native and immigrant workers. Although purely speculative, this explanation would also be consistent with the fact that the USA is the only country in which people are more worried about competition in the labour market than about crimes committed by immigrants (Figure 1.3).

I.4   TRENDS IN IMMIGRATION AND CRIME RATES

Using relative incarceration rates between immigrants and natives to measure their relative propensity to commit crimes is problematic because the probability of being incarcerated conditional on having committed a crime may differ substantially between immigrants and natives. For instance, foreigners may be subject to additional restrictions that prevent them from taking advantage of alternatives to prison, such as home detention.[7]

For this reason, we next move to crimes reported by the police as a better measure of criminal activity. Unfortunately, most countries do *not* report separate statistics for native and foreign offenders. Still, it is possible to investigate the effect of immigration on crime by looking at how overall crime rates change with the size of the immigrant population across geographical areas and over time. Indeed, this is the approach adopted by most country studies; see, e.g. Butcher and Piehl (1998) for the USA, Bianchi et al. (2012) for Italy, and Bell et al. (2013) for the UK. We extend the same approach to investigate the relationship between immigration and crime across OECD countries.

The OECD provides yearly series on the number of foreign-born residents during the period 2001–12. We combine these data with criminal statistics obtained from Eurostat (for the case of European countries) and from the national statistical offices (for OECD countries outside Europe). The resulting dataset includes complete series

---

[7]   Chapter 2 provides an extensive discussion of these issues for the case of Italy.

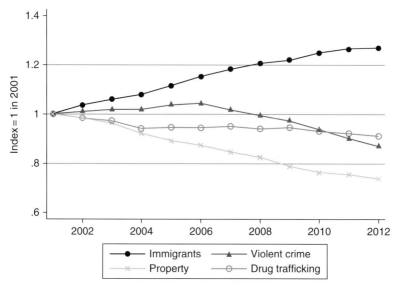

FIGURE 1.8 Trends in immigration and crime in the OECD, 2001–12.

on the total number of crimes reported by the police, further distinguished into the following categories: homicides, total violent crimes, drug offenses, total property crimes, robberies, domestic burglary, and motor vehicle theft. The final sample is a balanced panel of nineteen countries – all main countries in Western Europe plus Australia, Canada, New Zealand, and the USA – over twelve years.

Figure 1.8 preliminarily plots the evolution of immigration and (different types of) crime in the entire geographical area considered. All series are set equal to 1 in 2001. It appears clearly that immigration and crime rates follow opposite trends during the sample period. In particular, the share of immigrants over the total resident population increased by 27% while property crime rates decreased by exactly the same amount. Violent crimes and drug offences also decreased, although to a lesser extent.

In addition, Figure 1.9 shows there is no clear relationship between changes in immigration and crime rates across countries. The sign of the univariate correlation is sometimes positive and sometimes negative, depending on the type of offence, and the magnitude is

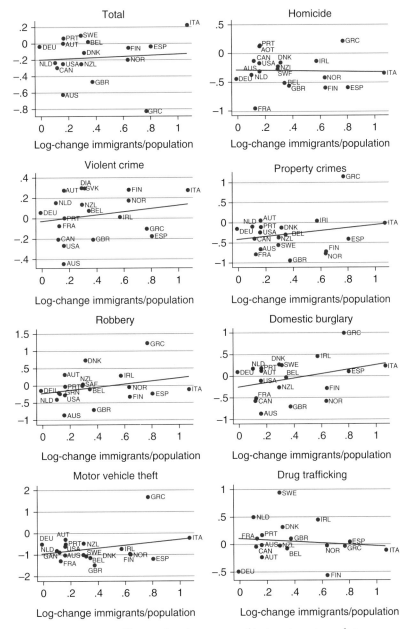

FIGURE 1.9 Changes in crime rates and in immigrant populations over the period 2001–12.

always very weak. Statistically, there is no measurable relationship between immigration and crime, and variation in immigration rates across countries explains almost none of the international differences in crime rates. Overall, cross-country analysis produces no evidence that crime rates correlate positively with immigration.

Of course, the univariate relationship between immigration and crime rate may depend on several factors in addition to the change in crime rates caused by immigration. For instance, positive economic shocks could attract more migrants to the OECD countries and at the same time reduce crime rates; the opposite would be true of course for negative economic shocks. This would induce a negative correlation between immigration and crime, but one that would not be particularly meaningful. Similarly, the univariate relationships in Figure 1.9 may largely reflect the long-run trends of the two variables. In particular, the homicide rate has been steadily decreasing in most countries during the past decades, whereas the evidence regarding other offences is less clear, possibly because of countervailing trends in reporting rates.

To take some of these issues into account, we move to multivariate regression analysis. In particular, we estimate the following equation:

$$\ln(\text{Crime}_{it}) = \beta \ln(\text{Migr}_{it}) + x_{it}'\gamma + f_i + f_t + \varepsilon_{it}, \quad (1.1)$$

where Crime_{it} is the crime rate in country i and year t, for different types of offences; Migr_{it} is the number of immigrants over the total resident population; x_{it} is a vector of other determinants of the crime rate; f_i and f_t are country- and year-specific fixed effect, respectively; and ε_{it} is an error term incorporating the effect of other determinants of the crime rate. Because the dependent and the main explanatory variables enter the equation in logarithms, the coefficient of main interest β is the estimated elasticity of the crime rate to the immigration rate, i.e. the percent increase in the crime rate associated, on average, with a 1% increase in the ratio of immigrants over the total population. Importantly, the properties of logarithm imply that differences in under-reporting of crimes and immigrants that are constant within countries (over time) and within periods (across countries) will not affect the estimated coefficient of interest; they are absorbed, respectively, by country and year fixed effects.[8]

Estimates of the elasticity of crime to immigration, for different types of offence and different specifications of Eq. (1.1), are reported in Table 1.1. The main message of multivariate regression analysis is similar to that of the univariate correlations in Figure 1.9: overall, there is no strong relationship between the evolution of immigration and (any type of) crime over time. In particular, when we simply allow for average, but constant, differences across countries in part A of Table 1.1 (e.g. with all else equal, the crime rate in Sweden would be 90% of the crime rate in the UK in every year) there is a negative relationship between immigration and the total number of crimes per capita. This finding reflects a negative correlation with property crimes and homicides, whereas there is a positive correlation with drug-related offences. However, all these correlations may reflect long-run trends in immigration and crime (e.g. the secular decrease in homicides). Indeed, coefficients are generally small and non-significant when controlling for common trends through the inclusion of year fixed effects (e.g. crime and immigration might be 5% lower in all countries in 2014 compared with 2015), as we do in part B of Table 1.1. Finally, including additional control variables on the right-hand side of the equation – namely, log gross domestic product (GDP) per capita, total unemployment rate, and youth unemployment – does not significantly affect the results (part C of Table 1.1).

The evidence in Table 1.1 can hardly be the last word on the (lack of) effects of immigration on crime for at least three reasons. Although the inclusion of fixed effects and additional control variables should reduce the scope for omitted variable bias, it is still

[8]   Bianchi et al. (2012) discuss this approach.

Table 1.1 *Immigration and crime in OECD countries, 2002–13*

	(1) Total	(2) Property	(3) Burglary	(4) Car theft	(5) Robberies	(6) Violent	(7) Murders	(8) Drugs
A: Country fixed effects								
Percentage change in crime associated with a 1% change in immigration	−0.259 (0.171)	−0.308 (0.341)	0.141 (0.262)	−0.843 (0.533)	0.029 (0.283)	0.143 (0.093)	−0.343* (0.174)	0.303* (0.172)
R^2	0.109	0.054	0.012	0.140	0.001	0.048	0.069	0.100
B: Country fixed effects and year fixed effects								
Percentage change in crime associated with a 1% change in immigration	0.138 (0.161)	0.241 (0.360)	0.367 (0.316)	0.529 (0.517)	0.236 (0.347)	0.134 (0.121)	0.207 (0.221)	0.258 (0.267)
R^2	0.349	0.197	0.069	0.468	0.032	0.141	0.238	0.130
C: Country fixed effects, year fixed effects, and additional control variables								
Percentage change in crime associated with a 1% change in immigration	0.186 (0.158)	0.154 (0.430)	0.248 (0.348)	0.552 (0.640)	0.009 (0.417)	0.140 (0.148)	0.248 (0.239)	0.334* (0.189)
R^2	0.460	0.248	0.191	0.472	0.156	0.157	0.256	0.234

$^*p < 10\%$; $^{**}p < 5\%$; $^{***}p < 1\%$.

possible that the (non-significant) estimated coefficient masks heterogeneous effects across countries. Indeed, the effect of immigration on crime may vary depending on the composition of the immigrant population in each country. Analogously to what happens for non-immigrants, the propensity of a given group to engage in crime varies strongly with the group (average) characteristics in terms of gender, age, and socio-economic status. However, immigrants differ among themselves in terms of another, important determinant of criminal behaviour: legal status.

Legal status allows immigrants to work in the official economy or start a new economic activity. Moreover, in most destination countries regular immigrants are entitled to social assistance and welfare payments. For all these reasons, they should enjoy higher legitimate income opportunities – and thus a greater opportunity cost of committing crimes – relative to undocumented immigrants.

In the next chapters, we examine the relationship among immigration, legal status, and crime in three countries: Italy, the UK, and the USA.

2 Migration Policy and Crime in Italy

In this chapter, we examine the relationship between immigration and crime in Italy, focusing in particular on the importance of legal status for the propensity of immigrants to engage in crime. In Section 2.1, we briefly describe the characteristics of the immigrant population in Italy and the evolution of Italian migration policy. Section 2.2 discusses the evidence on immigrants' involvement in crime in Italy. Finally, Section 2.3 discusses some estimates of the effect of legal status on outcomes, exploiting major legalization episodes in Italy during the past few decades.

2.1 MIGRATION POLICY IN ITALY

Immigration in Italy is a relatively recent phenomenon. Figure 2.1 shows that immigration started only at the end of the 1980s, increasing substantially after the collapse of the Soviet Union.[1] Between 1990 and 1999 the number of regular immigrants, as measured by the number of foreigners holding a valid residence permit, doubled from about 500,000 to 1 million (1% to 2% of the total population), mostly as a result of immigration from Eastern European countries. The influx of immigrants continued to accelerate during the following decade, bringing the number of residence permits to 3.9 million at the beginning of 2014. The number of foreigners reported in municipal registries (*anagrafe*) is even higher – 4.9 million – because it includes immigrants from new EU member countries, who no longer need a residence permit to stay in Italy. Overall, since the early 1990s the number of official foreign residents increased by about eight times.

---

[1] See Del Boca and Venturini (2003) for an analysis of emigration and immigration patterns in Italy.

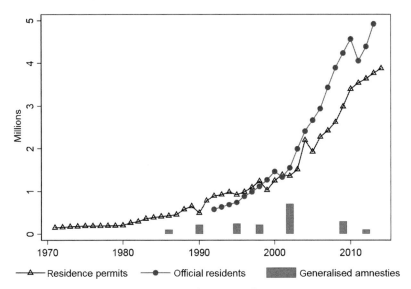

FIGURE 2.1 Immigrant population in Italy, 1971–2014.

Note: The continuous lines show the numbers of documented immigrants, as measured respectively by the number of residence permits (triangles) and official residents (circles). The bars report the number of applications received in each generalized amnesty.
Source: Elaborations from ISTAT and Ministry of Interior data.

Further, these figures likely under-estimate the actual increase in immigration, as they neglect a large number of irregular immigrants who entered Italy unofficially or overstayed temporary visas. Although it is difficult to measure the presence of undocumented immigrants, the numerous amnesties conducted in Italy during the past decades provide an important opportunity to gauge the size of irregular migration. On these occasions, immigrants who reside irregularly in Italy, and meet some broad conditions, can obtain a residence permit. The number of applications received during generalized amnesties provides a conservative estimate of the number of irregular immigrants who are present in the country. Figure 2.1 shows that seven general amnesties were launched between 1986 and 2012. Each of these amnesties involved a large number of applicants, reaching half of the officially recorded immigrant population in 2002.

We next discuss in detail the procedures for immigrants' entry in Italy (either through migration quotas or generalized amnesties).

2.1.1   The Quota System: Theory and Practice

Since the early 1990s, Italy has repeatedly attempted to set up a quota system to manage the legal inflows of migrant workers. This system was finally implemented in 1998 with the Turco–Napolitano law, later followed by the Bossi–Fini law of 2002 (see Appendix 1: Italian Legislation on Migration).

Each year the government establishes the number of immigrants allowed to enter the country in the following year for working purposes (both for seasonal and non-seasonal jobs) through 'Flows decrees' (in Italian: *Decreto Flussi*).[2] Each province is attributed a quota of immigrants, and special quotas are reserved for immigrants from countries that signed bilateral agreements to control irregular immigration with the Italian government. The quotas themselves vary year to year, and the Italian government can set an entry quota equal to zero in any given year, or allow access only to seasonal workers.

Once the 'Flows Decree' is approved and becomes effective, potential employers can apply to hire immigrant workers from different countries until the relevant quota is reached. According to the law, these immigrant workers should be recruited from abroad and should not be already residing in the country. When applying for an immigrant employee within the quota system, the employer can either request a specific individual (in Italian: *chiamata nominativa*) or hire the first person in the lists of job-seekers that are compiled by Italian embassies and consulates in each origin country.

---

[2]   To produce the yearly estimates of the number of new foreign workers needed from abroad – by region and by type (seasonal/non-seasonal) – the Italian government usually collects information from three main sources: (1) the National Institute of Statistics (ISTAT), regarding demographic trends of the Italian population and the decrease of the working population; (2) the Union of Chambers of Commerce, which annually provides an estimate of the additional immigrant workforce to be included in the labour market; (3) different studies on the state of the Italian productive system (European Migration Network, 2015).

In 2007 the application process was digitized, inaugurating what became known as 'click-days'. On these particular days, non-Italian applicants can download, fill in, and submit online requests to enter the country to work. Once the application has been positively assessed, the candidate for the working permit and her potential employer are summoned by the Italian authorities to sign the employ-ment contract and receive the residence permit, if granted. The intro-duction of click-days saved applicants from having to queue for hours outside the offices devoted to the collection of the application forms, but also made patently evident the randomness of the system. As we will discuss later in this chapter, a few minutes (or seconds) difference in filing the application online can now create a drastic reduction in the probability of obtaining legal status.

In spite of the fact that Italian policymakers usually refer to the quota system as a mechanism to allow the entry of new workers – as intended by the legislation – the reality is quite far from that (Ambrosini, 2011). Similar to an amnesty, the quota system is in practice mainly used to ex post legalize the existing (but undeclared) employment of undocumented immigrants who are already residing in Italy. In general, foreign workers first enter the Italian labour mar-ket as undocumented immigrants (or with a tourist visa); start work-ing unofficially; and then, if the employer is willing to sponsor them, wait for the 'Flows Decree' to legalize their position. Therefore, the main difference between the 'Flows Decrees' and an amnesty is that the former procedure has a cap on the number of legalized individuals (the annual quotas) while the latter does not.

The current design of the Italian quota system has two major limitations. First, it allows employers to hire only foreign workers who (in theory) are still residing abroad, implying that the match between employers and employees should occur from a distance.[3]

---

[3]   The 1998 Turco–Napolitano law, which introduced the quota system in Italy, also
      envisaged the possibility of legally accessing the Italian labour market as a job-searcher
      (the so-called sponsor institute). However, this possibility has been abolished by the
      2002 Bossi–Fini law.

Second, year-to-year uncertainty about the size of the quotas inevitably hinders firms' strategies of foreign recruitment. This is especially true when the quotas are binding, which occurs frequently (Fasani, 2010).

Furthermore, some specificities of the Italian context interact with the weaknesses of the quota system and lead to the actual malfunctioning of migration policy (Fasani, 2013). First, potential employers of foreign workers are mainly households or small firms, both of which give substantial value to personally knowing their potential employees and have relatively limited capability to engage in hiring from abroad.[4] Second, immigrant workers in Italy are demanded mostly for low-skilled, manual, and domestic care occupations: such skills are, in general, hardly certifiable and verifiable at a distance. Third, the size of the underground economy – generally estimated to be well above that in most other European countries – creates an optimal environment for the market for foreign workers to take place outside the existing legal framework (Reyneri, 2003).

Overall, because of these features of Italian immigration policy, there is a general consensus among practitioners and researchers that many immigrants enter Italy unofficially. These irregular immigrants subsequently try to obtain legal status, through either a working permit on 'click days' or a generalized amnesty.

2.1.2   Amnesties

Italy has historically used frequent general amnesties to ex post regulate the presence of immigrants in its territory and compensate for the absence of an adequate legal framework to manage inflows of immigrants. Indeed, three amnesties in 1986, 1990, and 1995 granted legal status to 105,000, 210,000, and 240,000 immigrants, respectively. As discussed in Section 2.1.1, in 1998 Italy reformed its

---

[4]   Italian firms are generally small; 95% of the 4.5 million Italian firms have fewer than 10 employees and account for almost 50% of the employed workers. Moreover, Italy has one of the lowest average numbers of employees per firm in Europe. In 2010, the figure was at 4 employees per firm, as compared to the EU27 average of 6.2. Below Italy are only Portugal (around 4) and Greece (3.3).

migration policy and adopted a quota system to manage inflows of foreign-born workers. However, amnesties were not abandoned: four more general amnesties followed (in 1998, 2002, 2009, and 2012), involving about 1.1 million immigrants in total.[5] Interestingly enough, Italian amnesties were launched under governments of all political orientations, including the so-called 'technical governments'. The first two amnesties (1986 and 1990) were granted by centrist governments, the third one by the 'technical government' led by Lamberto Dini in 1995. An additional amnesty was then granted by a left-wing government (in 1998), followed by two more procedures implemented by right-wing governments (in 2002 and 2009), and the last one by Mario Monti's 'technical government' in 2012. Overall, about 1.7 million immigrants have received legal status through one of these procedures.

Italy is not the only European country that has extensively used amnesties as a form of immigration control. Spain, for instance, granted six general amnesties in roughly the same span of time. And regularization processes also took place between 1980 and 2008 in Austria, France, Greece, and Portugal (Casarico, Facchini, and Frattini, 2012). This is quite different from the case of the USA, where the only general amnesty occurred in 1986 (see Chapter 4).

The contribution of amnesties to the numbers of documented immigrants in Italy is depicted in Figure 2.1. The number of applications increased from 105,000 in 1986 to 200,000 to 250,000 thousand in the three amnesties conducted during the 1990s. Applications peaked at 700,000 in 2002 – the largest Italian amnesty ever – then decreased to 300,000 in 2009 and 105,000 in 2012.

Although the undocumented population is hard to measure further in time from amnesty episodes, one can expect amnesties to have produced a roller-coaster trend in the years since the mid-1990s. In particular, general amnesties should substantially reduce the number

---

[5]   The 2009 amnesty was limited to domestic and care workers employed by families, while all the other allowed both firms and households to legalize their foreign-born employees.

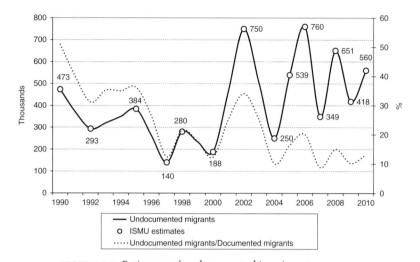

FIGURE 2.2 Estimates of undocumented immigrants, 1990–2010.

Note: The dots correspond to estimates of the number of undocumented immigrants residing in Italy produced by the ISMU Foundation. The dotted line reports the ratio of undocumented immigrants over documented immigrants residing in Italy in each year (vertical axis on the left).
Source: Elaborations from ISTAT and ISMU data.

of undocumented immigrants in the immediate aftermath of the process. At the same time, in the absence of a drastic change in migration policy, we can expect this population to start growing again immediately after the amnesty, and possibly at an even faster pace than it would have done otherwise, due to the recall effect of the amnesty. The ISMU foundation has produced estimates of the undocumented population since 1990, which are also reported in Figure 2.2.[6] The dotted line reports the ratio between the (estimated) undocumented population and the legal population. While the fluctuations reflect changes in the number of unauthorized immigrants, the overall

---

[6] The ISMU (Iniziative e Studi sulla Multietnicità) Foundation is an autonomous and independent organization promoting studies, research, and projects on multiethnic and multicultural society, focusing in particular on the phenomenon of international migrations (www.ismu.org). Since 2001, the ISMU Foundation has run an annual survey interviewing a representative sample of about 8,000 documented and undocumented migrants residing in the Lombardy region.

downward trend is the result of the gradual increase in the number of regular migrants, observed in Figure 2.1. The 470,000 undocumented immigrants estimated in 1990 were half the number of legal immigrants present in Italy at that time, whereas 560,000 undocumented immigrants in 2010 corresponded to just 13% of the number of legal immigrants. Therefore, even if the number of undocumented immigrants has increased over time, it has become less relevant relative to the legal resident population. As expected, the estimates also show substantial fluctuations in the number of undocumented immigrants, which corresponds with the passage of the regularization programs. As we will discuss in Chapter 4, the picture is quite different in the USA, where the last amnesty was enacted in 1986 and by most estimates the number of undocumented immigrants has increased since then, leading to the current number of 11 to 12 million.[7]

2.2 IMMIGRANTS' INVOLVEMENT IN CRIME

In 2011, immigrants to Italy accounted for a stunning 43% of individuals entering jail and for 36% of the number of inmates, whereas they represented about 7% of the resident population. Even if we add the estimated 560,000 undocumented immigrants who were residing in Italy in 2010 according to ISMU (see Figure 2.2), the picture would not change in any interesting way: the total immigrant population would account for about 8% of the resident population, but the substantial over-representation among the prison population remains. In particular, the percentage of incarcerated foreigners is highest among individuals charged for simple property crimes such as burglaries and larcenies as well as among violent offenders, whereas it is lowest among individuals charged for 'complex' crimes such as frauds and bank robberies (see Figure 2.3).

These figures are often used to support the claim that immigration increased crime in Italy. Notwithstanding, there is no evidence that crime has increased in Italy since the 1990s – when immigration

[7] Passel and Cohn (2008) estimate that in 2008 alone, the United States received about 500,000 new unauthorized immigrants.

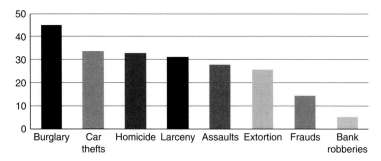

FIGURE 2.3 Percentage of foreigners among individuals charged for several types of crime.

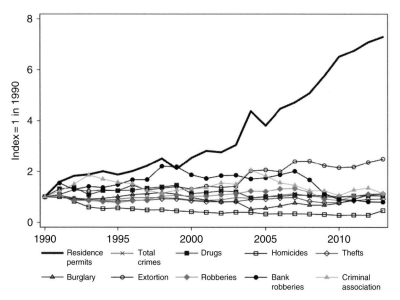

FIGURE 2.4 Trends in immigration and crimes, 1990–2013 (index = 1 in 1990).

Italy began to increase. During this period the ratio of immigrants to the total population increased by an order of magnitude, while the crime rate for most types of offences remained constant or even declined (see Figure 2.4). Therefore, the spectacular increase in immigration since the early 1990s was not accompanied by an increase in crime – if anything, the incidence of some serious crimes, such as

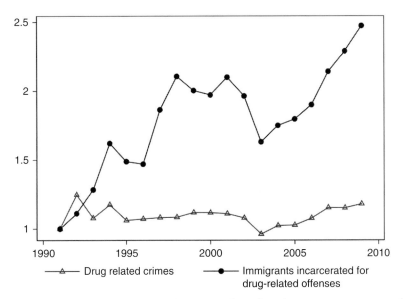

FIGURE 2.5 Drug-related crimes and number of immigrants incarcerated for drug-related offences since 1991 (index = 1 in 1991).

homicides, bank robberies, and thefts, declined during the same period.[8] This evidence is consistent with a very low elasticity of crime with respect to immigration, at least at the national level.[9]

How is it possible to reconcile the evidence in Figure 2.4 with the over-representation of immigrants in Italian prisons? One potential explanation is the substitution of native with foreign offenders in some types of criminal activities. To the extent that there are a limited number of criminal opportunities available in a given period, an increase in the number of crimes committed by immigrants would cause a parallel reduction in those committed by natives. This is indeed apparent in some specific illicit businesses such as drug-dealing. Until the late 1990s, this market was firmly in the hands of Italian criminal organizations, but nowadays it is largely under the control of foreign

---

[8]   The only clear exception in this respect is extortion, which is typically committed by (native) mafia-type organizations in Southern Italy.

[9]   Bianchi et al. (2012) confirmed these findings after taking into account the endogeneity of immigrants' flows.

organizations (Italian Ministry of Interior, 2007). However, the amount of drug consumption has not changed much during the period, likely because the demand for drugs does not obviously depend on the nationality of sellers. Indeed, Figure 2.5 shows that the number of drug-related crimes remained approximately constant, in spite of a 150% increase in the number of immigrants incarcerated for drug-related offences.

More generally, immigrant offenders may have substituted for natives in some types of criminal activities, in the same way as immigrant workers substituted for natives in some legal occupations such as domestic services. This explanation would reconcile the over-representation of immigrants in prison with the absence of significant effects on the crime rates – in spite of the eight-fold increase in immigration observed since the early 1990s.

Another important aspect to consider is that the relative incarceration rate between immigrants and natives may overstate their relative (unobserved) crime rate, as immigrants may be more likely to be incarcerated than natives, conditional on their actual involvement in crime. In principle, this could arise from discrimination against immigrants on the part of the police and the justice system[10]; or from a generally weaker position in courts, due to limited knowledge of language and local legislation; or from lesser access to alternative measures to incarceration, such as home detention. In 2011, 30.7% of the Italians convicted with prison sentences were assigned alternative measures, while for immigrants this figure was down to 12.7%. This is primarily due to the fact that immigrants often do not fulfil the conditions required by Italian courts to apply for alternatives to detention, which generally include having a regular job, having a domicile, having a family

---

[10]   We are not aware of any systematic study of discrimination of immigrants in the Italian judicial system. For the USA, recent empirical evidence shows that minorities tend to be disadvantaged in court, being either more likely to receive a sentence, or to receive longer sentences, or both (see, among others, Mustard, 2001 and Abrams et al., 2012).

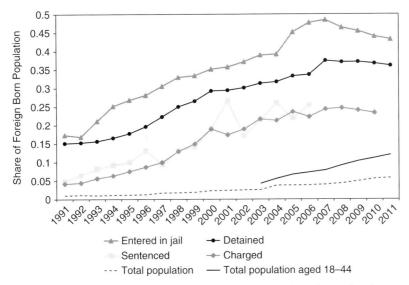

FIGURE 2.6 Share of foreign-born population in the Italian judicial system, 1991–2011.

Note: Elaborations from data of the Italian Minister of Internal Affairs and Minister of Justice. This figure extends by six years (2006–11) an otherwise similar figure in Fasani (2018).

able to host the individual, etc. Indeed, when we focus on charges and convictions as an alternative indicator of involvement in crime, the fraction of immigrants declines to about 20% (see Figure 2.6). This is significantly lower than the fraction of foreigners in prison, suggesting that the latter may overstate immigrants' involvement in criminal activity. At the same time, however, it is still higher than the share of foreign residents in the total population.

Finally, when comparing involvement in crime among immigrants and natives it is important to consider that the age distribution differs dramatically across the two groups. Figure 2.7 plots the share of foreign-born population by age and gender in Italy in 2011; the straight horizontal line corresponds to the overall (i.e. irrespective of age) immigrant share over the total population. Immigrants are strongly over-represented among the newborns (immigrant have higher

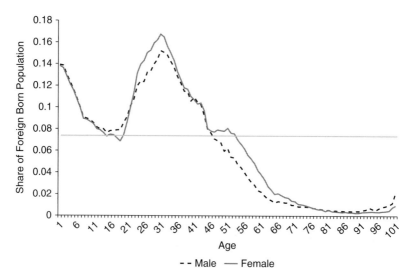

FIGURE 2.7 Share of foreign-born population, by age and gender, 2011.
Note: Elaborations from ISTAT data.

fertility rates than natives) and among people between 20 and 40 years old, reaching a peak of 15% to 17% of people in their early thirties. By contrast, immigrants are substantially under-represented among the population aged 55 and older. Given that the propensity to engage in crime also peaks at younger ages, differences in the demographic composition of natives and immigrants explain an important component of differences in crime rates.

To take into account differences in the demographic composition of the two groups, Figure 2.8 compares the age-specific probabilities of receiving a sentence for the foreign-born and for Italian citizens (in 2006). These probabilities are computed as the ratio of the number of convictions over the total number of residents in Italy. Such a ratio overestimates the probability of immigrants committing a crime because of the under-counting of undocumented immigrants at the denominator. With this caveat in mind, immigrants are greatly over-represented among offenders in all age categories. In particular, they are three to thirteen times more likely to receive a sentence, this

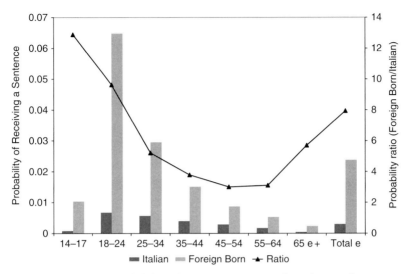

FIGURE 2.8 Probability of receiving a sentence for Italians and immigrants, by age group, 2006.

Note: Elaborations from data of the Italian Minister of Internal Affairs.

probability ratio being highest for the very young. This can be explained by the role that families can play in reducing incentives to commit crime (by providing income support) and limiting the severity of sanctions when accused (for instance, by paying for a good lawyer); immigrants have weaker family ties in Italy than do native Italians.

Overall, this evidence suggests that the demographic composition of the immigrant population and the higher probability of being incarcerated conditional on having committed a crime may be important determinants of the disproportionate presence of immigrants in Italian criminal statistics, but alone they cannot explain the difference in offending relative to natives. We next turn to the role of legal status.

2.3 LEGAL STATUS AND CRIMINAL BEHAVIOUR OF IMMIGRANTS IN ITALY

Undocumented immigrants in Italy can neither work nor start a business in the official economy. They can be employed in the

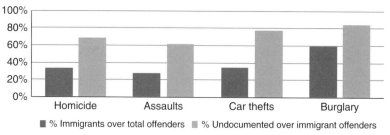

FIGURE 2.9 Immigrant status and legal status of offenders, by type of crime.

shadow economy, but in this case they face worse income opportunities and working conditions than in official labour markets. In addition, they are constantly at risk of being apprehended by the police and expelled by migration authorities, regardless of their criminal behaviour. As a result, undocumented immigrants could be generally characterized as having a lower opportunity cost of committing crime (and thus, a higher propensity to engage in it).

Unfortunately, it is hard to measure the crime rate of undocumented immigrants, as neither the number of unofficial residents nor the number of offenders among them is reported in official statistics. We can still approximate the crime rate, by the perpetrator's legal status, by exploiting information provided in an official report of the Italian Ministry of Interior (2011). In particular, the report provides the share of foreign immigrants and the share of the undocumented among all individuals charged for some types of crime, namely homicides, assaults, car thefts, and burglaries (see Figure 2.9).

Based on these data, we can estimate the representation of official and undocumented immigrants among offenders, relative to their incidence among total residents. Of course, to calculate precisely the extent of over-representation, we would need to know the number of undocumented immigrants, which is typically unobserved. Still, Figure 2.10 plots the implied over-representation of official and undocumented immigrants among offenders (on the vertical axis)

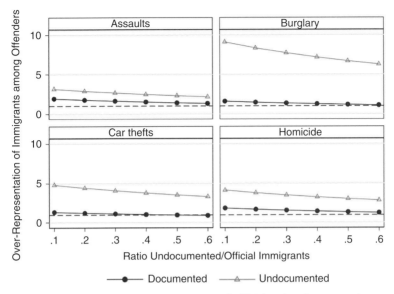

FIGURE 2.10 Over-representation of official and undocumented immigrants among offenders.

conditional on the ratio of undocumented to official foreign residents (on the horizontal axis).

The incidence of undocumented immigrants among offenders is several times larger than their presence among total residents, especially for property crimes. By contrast, legal immigrants are only slightly over-represented among offenders. Assuming the ratio of undocumented over total immigrant residents is around 50 to 60% (the same ratio observed at the time of the last generalized amnesty), legal immigrants would not be over-represented among offenders. It is also possible that conditional on differences in the demographic composition of (official) immigrants and natives (see Section 2.2), the former group would be less prone to crime than natives – although it is impossible to verify this conjecture without detailed individual-level data for immigrant and native offenders.

Therefore, the (disproportionately) high involvement of immigrants in crime seems entirely due to the undocumented, whereas regular immigrants exhibit a similar – or even lower – propensity to commit crimes as natives. This could be due in turn to the fact that obtaining legal status *causally* lowers the probability of committing crimes or, alternatively, that undocumented immigrants are *negatively selected* in terms of propensity to commit crimes. This distinction is very important for policy purposes: only in the former case would concession of legal status lower the crime rate of undocumented immigrants currently in the country. For this reason, we next explore these two alternative explanations for the difference in crime rates between official and undocumented immigrants.

2.3.1   Characteristics of Regular and Irregular Immigrants

Starting in 2001, the ISMU Foundation has been conducting an annual survey of immigrants in the Italian region of Lombardy.[11] The survey interviews a sample of about 9,000 individuals each year who are representative of all foreign immigrants in the region, *including the undocumented*. The sampling of undocumented immigrants is based on social networks around a number of 'aggregation centres' that are attended by all immigrants regardless of legal status (e.g. train stations, shops, and telephone centres); see Blangiardo (2008). Although undocumented immigrants could in principle try to hide their (illegal) status from interviewers, the available evidence suggests that this is not the case. For instance, the share of immigrants who declare to be illegally present in Italy in the ISMU survey is in line with estimates of the share of undocumented immigrants produced using alternative methods (e.g. applications for amnesty). Given the paucity of information about undocumented immigrants in official statistics, the

---

[11]   Lombardy is located in the northwest of Italy, and it is the largest of twenty regions in terms of both population and GDP (approximately 16% and 21% of the total, respectively). The region hosts more than 1 million (regular) immigrants, or one-fourth of all immigrants present in Italy. More information on the ISMU survey is available from the website of the Foundation, www.ismu.org.

Table 2.1 *ISMU survey (2003–09), characteristics of documented and undocumented immigrants*

	Documented	Undocumented	Diff.	St. diff.
Male	0.55	0.609	–0.059***	–0.12
	(0.003)	(0.006)	(0.006)	
Age	34.601	31.669	2.932***	0.33
	(0.049)	(0.099)	(0.11)	
Married	0.607	0.36	0.247***	0.51
	(0.003)	(0.005)	(0.006)	
Any children	0.598	0.421	0.176***	0.35
	(0.003)	(0.006)	(0.006)	
Number of children	1.238	0.87	0.368***	0.28
	(0.007)	(0.015)	(0.016)	
College education	0.158	0.121	0.037***	0.11
	(0.002)	(0.004)	(0.004)	
Employed	0.777	0.764	0.013**	0.03
	(0.002)	(0.005)	(0.005)	
Income (2005 euros)	1062.3	724.1	338.2***	0.49
	(4.4)	(7.3)	(9.7)	
Observations	33,763	8,237		

*$p < 10\%$; **$p < 5\%$; ***$p < 1\%$.

ISMU data constitute an important source of information on this group.[12]

Table 2.1 compares the individual characteristics of documented and undocumented immigrants. On average, the undocumented are younger and comprise a larger fraction of males. They also have a lower educational attainment and are less likely to be married or have children than documented immigrants. All these differences are sizable in magnitude and highly statistically significant.

The last rows of Table 2.1 show that undocumented immigrants also experience worse labour market outcomes, especially in

---

[12] Dustmann et al. (2017) have used the ISMU data to study the effect of immigrants' legal status on their consumption behaviour.

terms of salary (about 30% lower than official immigrants). This disadvantage reflects both the causal effect of legal status (i.e. the fact that undocumented immigrants can work only in the shadow economy) and the different composition of documented and undocumented immigrants (the latter group includes a larger fraction of young and low-skilled workers). For this reason, it is generally very difficult to isolate the causal effect of legal status from the endogenous selection of immigrants with different characteristics into one or the other group.

A similar argument holds when comparing the crime rate of official and undocumented immigrants. The higher involvement in crime by undocumented immigrants displayed in Figures 2.9 and 2.10 may reflect the causal effect of legal status – via worse labour market opportunities and, thus, a lower opportunity cost of committing crimes for undocumented immigrants – as well as the endogenous selection of immigrants into legal status. Indeed, all differences between the groups in Table 2.1 are strong predictors of criminal activity; young, single, low-skilled males are responsible for the vast majority of crimes (not only among immigrants); see Farrington (1986). In addition, documented and undocumented immigrants may also differ along unobservable dimensions. For instance, Dustmann et al. (2017) suggest that relatively less risk-averse individuals self-select into illegal status. Because criminals engage in extremely risky behaviour, we should expect them to have lower aversion to risk than non-criminals. Therefore, undocumented immigrants would likely exhibit a higher crime rate than other groups, on average, even in the absence of any causal effect of legal status on criminal behaviour.

2.3.2   The Causal Effect of Legal Status (I): Evidence from 'Click Days'

Pinotti (2017) exploited a peculiar feature of Italian migration policy to estimate the effects of legal status on immigrants' probability of committing crimes; the click days which allowed immigrants to apply for work authorization online. This research provides insight into the decision of the individual immigrant to commit offences.

As mentioned in Section 2.1.1, in 2007 the resident permit application process was completely digitized. From 2007 onwards, perspective employers submit applications starting at 8:00 a.m. of given click days of the year, and applications are processed based on the chronological order of arrival. If the application is accurate and complete, and the immigrant has no criminal record, he or she receives a residence permit; if instead, part of the information is missing, inaccurate, or false, or the applicant has a criminal record, the application is rejected. The process continues until the number of permits awarded exhausts the quota available for that lottery.

This mechanism generates a discontinuity in the probability of obtaining a residence permit at the cutoff time in which the last successful application is received, which in turn provides a particularly strong research design to estimate the causal effect of legal status on immigrants' behaviour. Comparing immigrants whose application was received just after the cutoff, and who were refused a residence permit due to the exhaustion of the quota, with immigrants whose application was received just before the cutoff and obtained the permit (conditional on the application being complete) mimics a random experiment. These two groups should be equal in all respects but legal status – due to a difference of a few minutes, or seconds, in the timing of the application. Therefore, we can attribute any difference in criminal behaviour in the period after the click days to the causal effect of legal status (as opposed to selection).

This empirical strategy, labelled *regression discontinuity* (RD), was pioneered by Thistlethwaite and Campbell (1960). As stressed by Lee and Lemieux (2010), and shown formally by Lee (2008), the RD framework allows for a clean identification of the effects of interest under the relatively mild condition that the agents are unable to *precisely* control the assignment near the cutoff. In other words, it is not necessary to assume away any selection into treatment. Instead, it is enough to assume that individuals who are very close to the cutoff

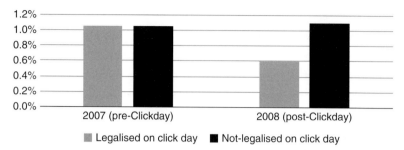

FIGURE 2.11 Probability of committing a serious crime before and after click day.

will not be able to *precisely* determine whether they end up just below or just above it (no matter how hard they try).

The implementation of the click days program matches the necessary conditions for causal identification in the RD framework very closely. Indeed, for all immigrants whose application was received close to the cutoff, it would be just a matter of luck whether they obtain or do not obtain a residence permit; how many fractions of a second sooner did they electronically submit their application relative to others? Moreover, in this specific case, the timing of the cutoff could not be known in advance, as it would ultimately depend on the timing of *all* applications, as well as on the fraction of those that were eventually rejected. These complexities provide a compelling argument for the assumption that legal status is as good as randomly assigned near the cutoff.

Figure 2.11 compares the probability of committing a serious crime in the year after the click day for immigrants applying just before and just after the cutoff, respectively. The probability of committing a crime decreases for immigrants legalized on click day by 0.5 percentage points – from 1.1% to 0.6% – relative to immigrants who did not obtain a residence permit.

To the extent that immigrants whose application was received just before and just after the cutoff are similar in all respects but for a few minutes (or seconds) in the timing of the application, we can attribute the difference in criminal behaviour to the causal effect of legal status. Indeed, additional evidence in Pinotti (2017) confirms that age, country of origin, and Italian province of destination are not significantly different between immigrants to the left and to the right of the cutoff. Of course, the two groups may differ along other dimensions. Unfortunately, our administrative data do not report any information on important determinants of criminal activity such as income and educational levels, and in any case some other confounding factors would be very hard to measure (e.g. attitudes towards illegal activities and risk aversion). Nevertheless, the fact that the characteristics that we do observe appear to not change across the application cutoff supports the assumption that legal status is as good as randomly assigned near the cutoff.

2.3.3 The Causal Effect of Legal Status (II): Evidence from Generalized Amnesties

The generalized amnesties that were frequently implemented in Italy during the past decades (see Section 2.1.2) provide a unique opportunity to estimate the causal effect of legal status – separately from selection and compositional effects. On such occasions, in fact, *all* immigrants who are illegally present in the country are offered the opportunity to apply for a residence permit under very benign conditions, so selection into legal status should be a lesser concern when comparing crime rates before and after the amnesty. For this reason, one can attribute changes in crime after the amnesty to the causal effect of legal status on the population of legalized immigrants.

As a matter of fact, Figure 2.12 suggests that amnesties in Italy are followed by reductions in the rate at which immigrants commit crime. We have plotted the total number of criminal charges of immigrants (per 10,000 population) for the period 1993 to 2005 for each of the 20 Italian regions. The increasing trend in all regions reflects the expansion of the foreign-born population discussed in the first part of this chapter. The vertical lines on the graphs signal the three general amnesties (1995–96; 1998–99; 2002–03) granted in this period. Although there is substantial heterogeneity across regions, one can

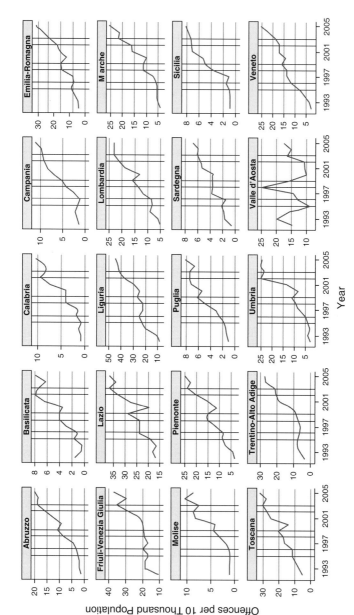

FIGURE 2.12 Immigrants' crime and amnesties, 1992–2005.

Note: The graph plots the total number of criminal charges of immigrants (per 10,000 population) for the period 1992–2005 for each Italian region. The vertical lines signal the three general amnesties granted in this period (1995–96; 1998–99; 2002–03).

notice that in amnesty years – or in the years immediately following an amnesty – regional crime rates of immigrants experienced a marked slow-down of the increasing trend, or even an absolute reduction.

Fasani (2018) empirically tested whether general amnesties in Italy led to reductions in the number of crimes committed by immigrants in Italy. He analyses records on criminal charges against immigrants over the period 1990–2005. In these years, four amnesties were enacted, legalizing 218,000 immigrants in 1990, 244,000 in 1995, 217,000 in 1998, and 637,000 in 2002. Fasani (2018) studied whether regions in which a higher share of immigrants obtained legal status experienced a greater decline in immigrant crime rates. To do so, he estimates panel regressions and exploit both the geographical variation in the number of immigrants legalized in different Italian regions and the time variation generated by the repeated programs. His estimates point at a statistically significant reduction in regional crime in the year following the amnesty, which is increasing in the share of undocumented immigrants who were legalized over the resident population (i.e. in the intensity of the 'legalization treatment'). This finding is not affected by the inclusion of regional controls (resident population, gross domestic product [GDP] per capita, unemployment rate, etc.) or different trends, and by the use of alternative measures of immigrant crime. These results confirm the visual evidence in Figure 2.12, where generalized amnesties of undocumented immigrants are followed by a marked decline in the number of crimes they commit in Italy.

To interpret such decline as a causal effect of legalization, however, one should be willing to assume that the number of undocumented immigrants legalized in each region and each amnesty is as good as random. In other words, there should not be omitted factors that are correlated with both regional crime and the number of legalizations. This assumption may be problematic, as undocumented immigrants have more incentives to apply for legal status in areas where potential benefits of legal status are higher, that is, in areas where unemployment rates are lower and formal labour markets offer better opportunities relative to the unofficial sector. If better employment opportunities lead to lower crime rates, we may then observe that regions that receive more amnesty applications (and legalize more immigrants) have less crime, even if there is no causal relationship between the two variables. Fasani (2018) addresses these concerns in three ways. First, by estimating panel regressions, he removes any persistent regional difference in labour market conditions, size of the shadow economy, overall crime rates, etc. by first differencing the data and exploiting within-region variation over time in legalizations and crime. Second, he includes time-varying regional controls – such as GDP per capita and unemployment rate – to absorb the local economic cycle that is potentially correlated with both the number of applications and the regional crime rate of immigrants. Third, he develops alternative instrumental variable strategies to deal with the potential endogeneity of the 'legalization treatment'. In particular, following Altonji and Card (1991), he constructs predicted measures of the number of immigrants legalized in each amnesty and each region based on past location choices of immigrants (in 1981 or 1990) and past amnesty application decisions of undocumented immigrants (in 1986). These alternative measures are then used to instrument the actual number of legalizations. By doing so, he exploits only exogenous variation in the number of legalized immigrants that is driven by local networks of previous immigrants who were legalized in the past – rather than by contemporaneous economic shocks (that may directly affect crime rates).[13] The estimates obtained by using these instrumental variables confirm the findings from ordinary least squares regressions: legalizing more undocumented immigrants in a region leads to a reduction in crime committed by immigrants.

The data on criminal charges contain the information on nationality of the offender, which allows distinguishing three groups: Italian citizens, non-EU immigrants, and EU immigrants. Over the period 1990–2005, these groups accounted on average for 87%, 12%, and 1%

---

[13]   This approach has been extensively used in immigration literature; see among others Card (2001), Ottaviano and Peri (2006), Dustmann et al. (2008), Bianchi et al. (2012), and Bell et al. (2013).

of the criminal charges, respectively. Amnesty programs in Italy are meant to grant legal residence status to non-EU immigrants, while they do not produce any direct effect on Italian and EU citizens. If anything, we should thus expect to observe an impact of legalizations on the criminal behaviour of non-EU immigrants but not on the behaviour of the other two groups. This is indeed what Fasani (2018) finds in his analysis: a significant crime-reduction effect is estimated exclusively for the potential beneficiaries of the policy, namely the non-EU immigrants.

As a matter of fact, if amnesties reduce the crime supply but leave crime demand unaffected, the criminal opportunities that are no longer taken by the legalized immigrants could be seized by other groups of potential offenders, for instance, by other groups of the migrant population and/or by native offenders. The lack of a significant effect of amnesties on the crime rate of natives and EU immigrants implies the absence of substitution effects in the criminal market across these subgroups of the resident population. Nevertheless, there may still substitution effects taking place within the non-EU immigrant population. Note that this latter group comprises migrants who were already legal residents before the amnesty, those who were legalized, those who remained undocumented (because they did not apply or were unsuccessful), and those who arrived (legally or illegally) after the amnesty ended. If legalized immigrants obtain access to better labour market opportunities and therefore experience a reduction in their incentives to commit crime, the other groups may take some of those 'unexploited criminal opportunities', increasing their own propensity to engage in crime. Unfortunately, the data used by Fasani (2018) do not allow distinguishing non-EU immigrant offenders by residence status. The estimated effect refers to the entire population group and, therefore, identifies the net effect of responses that may potentially go in opposite directions (i.e. negative for legalized immigrants and positive for the other subgroups).

To indirectly test whether the estimated reduction in immigrants' crime rates is driven by improved labour market opportunities for legalized immigrants, Fasani (2018) analysed heterogeneity across different macro areas of Italy. Indeed, if that is the mechanism at play, the crime-reducing effect of granting legal status should be stronger in areas that offer more and better working opportunities in the formal labour market. Consistent with this conjecture, Fasani (2018) estimates a larger elasticity of immigrant crime to the 'legalization treatment' in the Northern regions, which have a higher GDP per capita, lower unemployment, and smaller shadow economy than Central and Southern regions. In a similar way, Mastrobuoni and Pinotti (2015) find an effect of legal status on reincarceration rates exclusively in the North of Italy.

According to the estimates reported in Fasani (2018), almost doubling the number of undocumented immigrants in a region would imply a 20% reduction in the number of immigrants who receive a criminal charge. The magnitude of this effect is economically relevant (although not large) but short lived. In further estimates, indeed, Fasani (2018) studied the timing of the crime-reduction effect of amnesties and found that this effect vanishes two years after the legalization program was concluded.

The presence of substitution effects within the non-EU immigrant population – as discussed earlier – may potentially explain why this aggregate effect appears relatively smaller when compared to legalization effects estimated using individual data exclusively on legalized individuals, as in Mastrobuoni and Pinotti (2015) and Pinotti (2017). Moreover, even in the absence of substitution effects the inclusion of non-EU immigrants who were already documented – hence not affected by the amnesties – in the calculation of crime rates dilutes the estimated effect of the amnesty on the behaviour of the undocumented. Further, Fasani (2018) emphasizes that the magnitude and duration of the amnesty crime-reduction effect crucially depends on how effective legalizations are in reducing the presence of illegal residents in the country. In particular, the announcement of amnesties typically triggers sizeable inflows of new immigrants, increasing in turn the number of crimes committed by immigrants at the local level. This is particularly true if conditions of the amnesty prevent a significant proportion of these newcomers from obtaining legal status (see, for instance, Devillanova et al., 2018, on the 2002 Italian amnesty, or Freedman et al., 2018 for a similar evaluation of the 1986 US amnesty), so they will remain in the country with poor labour market prospects. Notably, the crime-reducing effect of the amnesty may be zero even in the short run, if newly legalized immigrants are immediately replaced by a new inflow of undocumented immigrants.

Overall, the empirical evidence based both on amnesty programs and on click days points at legal status playing a significant role in reducing immigrants' incentives to engage in crime. This empirical finding is fully consistent with the hypothesis that legal status improves immigrants' opportunities in the legal sector, making this option preferable to crime.

3 Immigration and Crime in the United Kingdom

3.1 INTRODUCTION

The UK is a major recipient of migrant inflows from both other European countries and the rest of the world. Unlike the Italian experience (see Chapter 2), immigration to the UK is not a new phenomenon; substantial numbers of foreign-born workers entered the UK in the 1960s and 1970s. In recent years, however, the number of immigrants to the UK has increased considerably, primarily as a consequence of EU enlargements in 2004 and 2007. These rapid changes, and the government's response to them, provide a very exciting setting to explore the immigration–crime link. Has the arrival of novel and large immigrant wave made the UK a more dangerous country in recent years? In this chapter, we address this empirical question by comparing aggregate trends in immigrant population and crime, by discussing judicial statistics, and by developing a novel econometric analysis of the impact of immigration on local crime rates.

The structure of the chapter is as follows. In Section 3.2, we describe recent developments in the British immigration policy, trends in numbers and flows of its immigrant population, and migrants' main nationalities and educational levels. Section 3.3 illustrates recent changes in the offending rate in the UK, distinguishing among different types of crimes. The involvement of immigrants in criminal activities in the UK is discussed in Section 3.4, where we analyse prison records of detained offenders. Finally, Section 3.5 addresses the important policy question of whether the presence of immigrants in an area leads to an increase in local crime rates. After reviewing previous research on the British context, we provide new empirical evidence on this issue. The chapter ends with some concluding remarks in Section 3.6.

3.2 IMMIGRATION IN THE UK: POLICY, NUMBERS, AND FLOWS

3.2.1 *Immigration Policy*

The UK has long been a destination country for migratory flows across the globe. Part of this history of immigration is due to the arrival of nationals from former British colonies and Commonwealth countries (e.g. India and Jamaica). Citizens of the former British Empire traditionally enjoyed free movement and settlement rights in the UK, although these entitlements were gradually restricted in the 1960s and 1970s. Free access was instead granted to Irish nationals and, increasingly over time, to European citizens.

The 'Conservative era' – lasting from 1980 to 1997 under the leadership of Margaret Thatcher and John Major – saw fairly limited inflows of immigrant workers. These relatively low levels of immigration were the consequence of restrictive immigration policies, economic recessions (in 1980–81 and 1990–91), and the absence of major push factors of international flows during most of the period. The fall of the Iron Curtain and the conflict in the former Yugoslavia in the mid-1990s resulted in an increase in the migratory pressure (asylum seekers in particular) on British borders.

Starting in 1997, the newly elected Labour government of Tony Blair pushed for a shift in UK immigration policy, in the direction of allowing more foreign-born workers to enter the country. One of the most relevant actions of this new policy regime was the decision to allow free access to the UK labour market to migrants from the ten 'New Member States' (NMS; Cyprus, the Czech Republic, Estonia, Hungary, Latvia, Lithuania, Malta, Poland, Slovakia, and Slovenia) that joined the EU in May 2004. In fact, the UK was one of only three EU countries – Ireland and Sweden being the other two – that allowed immediate free movement of EU8 workers across their borders. All the other EU countries adopted 'transitional periods' that allowed restricting labour market access of citizens from NMS for up to seven years (Boeri and Brücker, 2005). From May 2004, workers from NMS could move to the UK and were fully entitled to work there, being subject only to the obligation of registering on the Worker Registration Scheme (WRS) within one month of taking up employment in the UK.[1]

The decision to immediately open the borders, while other major potential destination countries in the UK kept their labour market shut, led to what is commonly considered the single largest immigration wave to the UK. The largest number of NMS migrants came from Poland, with more than 250,000 workers entering in the first two years after the enlargement, compared to a 2001 Polish-born population of around 60,000 (Drinkwater et al., 2009).

The UK government's posture towards immigration was notably different in the following EU enlargement. Indeed, when Romania and Bulgaria joined the EU in 2007 several restrictions were imposed on the ability of their citizens to work in the UK. In particular, Romanian and Bulgarian workers were essentially allowed only to be employed in the agricultural sector, or to be self-employed (Clark et al., 2014).

In 2008, the Labour government introduced a Points-Based System (PBS) to regulate economic and educational migrants from outside the European Economic Area (EEA). The PBS replaced the previous system of immigration by compressing what had previously been eighty work and study routes into the UK into five main 'Tiers' (Devitt, 2012). Given that unskilled workers could now freely arrive from the enlarged EU, the main intent of the PBS was to increase the

---

[1]   Drinkwater et al. (2009) suggest that WRS records likely underestimate the actual inflow of NMS citizens to the UK because some workers – especially those coming for short periods or seasonal work – may have failed to register. The WRS, however, measures the arrival of new workers but it does not capture return migration (unless all workers who are leaving the UK bother to de-register from the scheme, which is unlikely), potentially leading to an overestimation of the actual numbers of NMS workers.

average skill level of migrants from outside the EEA by awarding points to migrants for their English language ability and their educational qualifications. The PBS gives preference to immigrants who will work in a specific set of 'shortage occupations'. These occupations are identified by the Migration Advisory Committee (MAC), a non-departmental public body established in 2007 to provide independent advice to the government on immigration policy.

Immigration took central stage in the political debate that led to the UK general elections held in May 2010. The Conservative Party included in its platform the declared intention of radically curbing net immigration to the UK: '. . . we will take steps to take net migration back to the levels of the 1990s – tens of thousands a year, not hundreds of thousands' (Conservative Party, 2010, p. 21). The Conservative Party won the elections in 2010 and then again in May 2015. The target of reducing net immigration from the 'hundreds of thousands' to the 'tens of thousands' remained high on the political agenda of the British government. This target was reflected in stricter policies for admitting workers, non-EU students, and family members. The Conservative government reformed the PBS: some Tiers were shut down and others were capped.[2] In addition, closer scrutiny was given to colleges and schools that sponsor international students.[3] Further, family reunification was limited by considerably raising the income threshold required for British citizens and settled residents to be eligible for reunion with close family members.

---

[2] The newly elected government decided to close access through 'Tier 1 General', an entry channel that applied to highly skilled potential migrants looking for a job or wishing to become self-employed in the UK. The 'Tier 1 – Post Study Work' was also closed. Under that scheme, students from any nationality who had successfully obtained an undergraduate or postgraduate degree at a UK institution could apply for permission to work in the UK for two years. Further, a cap of 20,700 workers was imposed in 2011 on 'Tier 2 General', an employer-sponsored migration scheme reserved for skilled workers who hold a job offer from a UK-based employer.

[3] In response to this scrutiny, more than 800 colleges either failed to reapply for sponsor status under the new rules or had their license to sponsor non-EU students revoked. This led to a substantial drop in the number of visas issued to international students, decreasing from about 250,000 in 2010 to 200,000 in 2014.

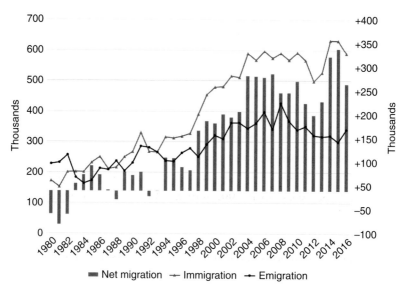

FIGURE 3.1 Immigration, emigration, and net immigration flows, 1980–2016.

Source: Authors' calculations based on UK Office for National Statistics Long-Term International Migration data.

As we will show in the next section, net immigration figures since 2010 have so far systematically proven that the government failed to meet its target of reducing immigration to 'tens of thousands a year'. Despite all efforts, net immigration remained above 200,000 per year until 2011; it dropped to 180,000 in 2012 and then peaked at more than 310,000 in 2014 (see Figure 3.1). The fact that the access of EEA nationals cannot be restricted using immigration policy – because they enjoy the free mobility associated with EU citizen status – became one of the arguments used to justify this failure. The persistently high levels of immigration into the UK were also widely used as an argument in support of a pro-'Brexit' vote in the referendum of June 2016, in which almost 52% of the voters opted for leaving the EU.

3.2.2   Numbers and Flows

Despite receiving sizeable immigrant inflows that date back to the 1960s and 1970s, the UK actually remained a country of net emigration until the mid-1980s, when it started having positive net immigration flows.[4] The UK Office for National Statistics (ONS) produces estimates of the number of individuals entering and leaving the country in each year (Long-Term International Migration [LTIM]).[5] Figure 3.1 reports estimates of immigration, emigration, and net immigration flows (vertical axis on the right) to and from the UK between 1980 and 2016. The graph shows that immigration flows clearly overtook emigration flows in 1993 and yearly net immigration has been positive since then. This net inflow remained below 100,000 individuals per year until 1997 (during the 'Conservative era'; see previous section); it reached approximately 150,000 per year between 1998 and 2004, and it increased again after 2004 to an annual inflow of more than 250,000 people. During the Great Recession that followed the 2008 financial crisis, both emigration and immigration flows slowed down. The drop in the inflow was more dramatic: net immigration dropped, reaching a minimum of approximately 180,000 net entries in 2012, back to the level observed before the 2004 EU enlargement. Net immigration peaked in 2015, hitting the unprecedented level of 332,000 net immigrants.

A consistent record of positive net immigration since 1994 has naturally led to a larger resident population, as well as a growing immigrant population in the UK. Figure 3.2 plots the evolution in the number of foreign-born residents and foreign nationals living in the UK from 2000 to 2017. Data come from the 2001 and 2011 Census and from the Annual Population Surveys (APS).[6] The dotted lines in the figures report foreign-born and foreign nationals as a share of total

4   See Hatton (2005) for an analysis of the determinants of this transition.
5   Although LTIM data are the official estimates used by the British government to measure national inflows and outflows, they suffer from two main limitations. First, the estimates relate only to long-term migration – those intending to stay in the UK for at least one year – which implies that they only partially cover the extent of migration to the UK. Second, given that the data are mainly obtained from a survey – the International Passenger Survey – that samples only a relatively small number of migrants, there are important concerns over the accuracy of the estimates.
6   Started in 2004, the Annual Population Survey (APS) is a continuous household survey, covering the UK. The topics covered include employment and unemployment, as well as housing, ethnicity, religion, health, and education. The APS is not a stand-alone

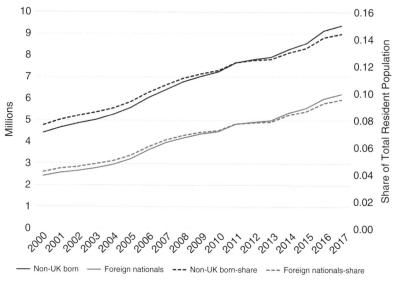

FIGURE 3.2 Foreign-born residents and foreign nationals in the UK, 2000–17.

Source: Authors' calculations based on UK Office for National Statistics data.

resident population. The non–UK-born population more than doubled over this period of time, experiencing a 112% increase from 4.4 million in 2000 to almost 9.4 million in 2017. As a share of total resident population, that of foreign-born citizens increased from 8% in 2000 to 14% in 2017. The time series of foreign nationals follows the same upward trend over the period considered, although the level is lower. Foreign citizens, indeed, numbered 2.4 million in 2000 (4% of the resident population) and 6.2 million in 2017 (10% of the resident population).

The lower number of foreign nationals relative to the number of foreign-born residents likely reflects the relative ease of acquiring British citizenship. In the UK, foreign-born individuals can be naturalized through marriage with a British citizen or after five years of

survey; it uses data combined from two waves of the main Labour Force Survey (LFS), collected on a local sample boost.

legal residence in the UK (plus one additional year as a 'settled resident'). Children may qualify for either automatic or discretionary 'registration' as British citizens depending on the country of their birth and the nationalities of their parents. Between 2000 and 2014, almost 2.3 million foreign residents were granted British nationality, an average of 150,000 per year (Home Office, 2016). Approximately half of these naturalizations were based on residence, a quarter were marriage-based grants, and the remaining quarter were minor child registrations.

Owing to this relatively automatic and straightforward procedure for naturalization, figures on foreign-born residents, rather than the number of citizens of other countries that reside in the UK, are generally used to measure the presence of immigrants in the UK. Throughout the chapter, we will refer to this time series unless otherwise specified.

3.2.3 Countries of Origin and Education

In the previous section, we documented the dramatic increase in the share of immigrants residing in the UK. We now discuss which important changes in the composition of their countries of origin took place in recent years. In Figure 3.3, we illustrate the composition of the foreign-born population by area of origin and its evolution over the period 2004–17. Throughout the period, Asian immigrants represent the largest group: their share over the total immigrant population remained constant at approximately one-third, although their number grew rapidly from 1.7 million in 2004 to 2.9 million in 2017. Over most of the period, the second largest group consisted of EU14 citizens, who increased from 1.2 million to almost 1.7 million, although their share declined from 23% to 18%. NMS citizens experienced a very fast growth after the EU enlargements: there were 271,000 such immigrants (5% of the immigrant population) in 2004, the year the first enlargement took place, a population that grew to more than 2 million in 2017 (accounting for 21% of the immigrant population). In 2014, NMS citizens overtook EU14 citizens and became the second

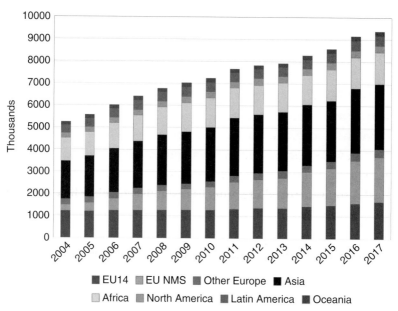

FIGURE 3.3 Foreign-born residents by area of origin, 2004–17.
Source: Authors' calculations based on UK Office for National Statistics data.

largest group of immigrants in the UK. Immigrants from Africa increased from 1 million to 1.4 million between 2004 and 2017, while their share of total immigrant population declined from 20% to 15%. Finally, immigrants from all other areas experienced small increases in absolute numbers and equally small declines in their shares. In 2017, they jointly accounted for approximately 15% of the foreign residents: 5% from Latin America, 4% from non-EU European countries, 3% from North America, and 2% from Oceania.

Table A.1[7] reports the first fifteen countries of origin of the foreign-born population residing in the UK in 2000 and in 2017. In 2000, Irish citizens were the largest national group (11% of the foreign-born population), followed by Indians (10%), Pakistanis (6%), Germans (5%), and Bangladeshi (4%). USA, Kenya, Jamaica, and

_____
[7]   All tables discussed in this chapter are provided in Appendix 2.

South Africa were at 3%, while Australia, China, Italy, France, Cyprus, and Sri Lanka were at 2%. The ranking in 2017 presents some notable novelties, along with some persistence. Polish citizens (10%) entered the ranking at the first place and Romanians (4%) in fourth position. India (9%) and Pakistan (6%) maintained their positions in second and third place, respectively, while the Republic of Ireland (4%) and the USA (2%) lost substantial ground.

How do immigrants in the UK compare in their educational attainments to migrant populations hosted in other European countries? A solid empirical literature has established a clear link between education and crime, showing that more educated individuals are less likely to offend (see, among others, Lochner and Moretti, 2004; Machin et al., 2011; Deming, 2011; Hjalmarsson et al., 2015.) These findings are consistent with an economic model of crime described by Becker (1968), whereby higher educational attainment improves legal labour market opportunities, reducing the incentives to engage in criminal behaviour. Education is also a key variable in facilitating the process of social and economic integration of migrants.[8] Better educated migrants are generally expected to find a job faster, and should be able to access better-paid occupations, both of which would lower their incentives to commit crime.

Figure 3.4 compares the shares of population aged 15 to 64 with tertiary education among natives and immigrants in EU15 countries, Norway, and Switzerland. The data refer to year 2015. In the graph, countries are ordered by share of foreign-born residents with tertiary education, from largest to smallest. With 48% of the immigrant population that is highly educated (relative to 35% of the natives), Ireland comes first in the ranking. The UK follows in second place: 47% of their immigrants (and 36% of natives) have achieved a tertiary education. These figures are in stark contrast with the EU15 average – 30% of foreign-born residents had tertiary education in 2015 – and with those of other major destination countries such as France (29%),

---

[8] See Dustmann and Glitz (2011) for a review of the literature on migration and education.

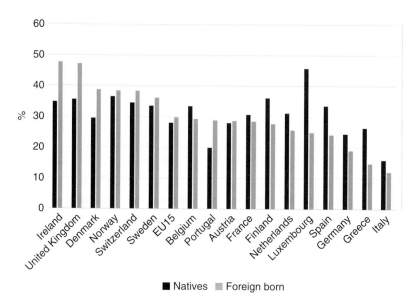

FIGURE 3.4 Share of population aged 15–64 years with tertiary education in EU15 countries + Norway + Switzerland: natives and foreign born, 2015.

Source: Authors' calculations based on Eurostat data.

Germany (19%), or Italy (12%). The educational level of immigrants in the UK, therefore, is substantially higher than in any other EU country (with the only exception of the Republic of Ireland).

3.3   CRIME TRENDS IN THE UK

Crime data in the UK primarily come from one of two sources: the Crime Survey for England and Wales (CSEW) and police recorded crime.[9] The Crime Survey for England and Wales (formerly British Crime Survey) is an annual victimization survey in which interviewees are asked about their experience of crime in the past twelve months, their perceptions regarding crime and safety in the area where they life, and their assessment on the work done by police and

---

[9]   Both sources are geographically limited to England and Wales. Separate crime records are collected in Scotland and Northern Ireland and they cannot be aggregated with records from England and Wales. They are not discussed in this chapter.

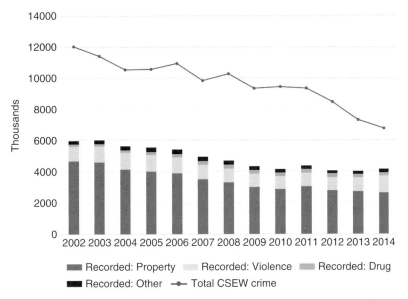

FIGURE 3.5 Trends in total CSEW crime and recorded crime, by offence group.

Source: Authors' calculations based on Home Office data.

judicial system The CSEW captures a broad range of victim-based crimes experienced by respondents, including those that were not reported to the police. Nevertheless, there are some serious but relatively low-frequency offences (e.g. homicide and sexual offences) that are not included in the estimates produced with CSEW data. The survey was first conducted in 1982 and ran at roughly two-year intervals until 2001, when it became an annual survey. The sample size is approximately 50,000 households. The second source of crime data in UK is based on crimes recorded by police forces in England and Wales. These data cover all offences reported to the police (which are a subset of total committed offences), of every type, and are the primary source for subnational crime statistics and for information on relatively serious, but low-volume, crimes that are poorly measured by a sample survey.

Figure 3.5 illustrates trends in the total number of offences in England and Wales from 2002 to 2014. The continuous line reports total crime as estimated from CSEW data: total offences experienced a 43% decline over this period, dropping from more than 12 million in 2002 to 6.7 million in 2014. Police-recorded crime – disaggregated by major type of offence – is displayed by the vertical bars. As discussed in the previous paragraph, recorded crime captures a subset of all committed crimes and is therefore well below CSEW crime: in the British context, recorded crime is generally 50% to 60% of total crime. Note that trends are very similar between the two time series, however.[10] Offences notified to the police declined by 30%, from almost 6 million in 2002 to 4.2 million in 2014. When looking at different crime types, we can see that property crime (minus 43% between 2002 and 2014) is driving this downward trend. The other three categories, instead, have all increased: Violence (+16%), Drug (+34%), and Other Offences (+13%).

The steep upward trend in immigrant population from 2000 to 2017 illustrated in Figure 3.2 is in stark contrast with the strong decline in criminal offences depicted in Figure 3.5 over the same period of time. These opposing trends suggest that immigration in the UK has not led to higher levels of crime in the country as a whole. On the contrary, crime rates kept declining even in periods – such as the post–2004 EU enlargement years – when the country was adjusting to unprecedentedly large inflows of foreign citizens. This conclusion, however, does not rule out the possibility that areas that attracted more substantial flows of foreign-born citizens experienced raises, or perhaps slower reductions, in their local crime rates. We will investigate this issue in Section 3.5.

3.4   IMMIGRANT CRIME IN THE UK: EVIDENCE FROM PRISON RECORDS

Judicial statistics disaggregated by nationality of the offender are systematically provided by the British government for convicted

---

[10]   This is not always the case; for example, US crime trends in victimization-based and police-based data sets diverged in the 1970s and 1980s, an anomaly that could be explained by changes in police practices that encouraged crime reporting.

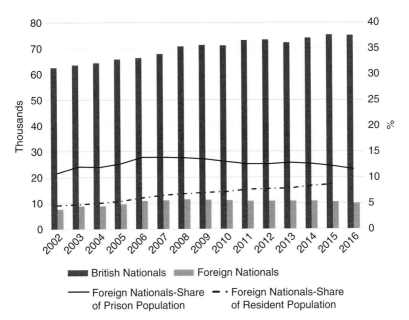

FIGURE 3.6 UK prison population by nationality, 2002–16.

Source: Authors' calculations based on Ministry of Justice data.

criminals who are held in detention in UK prisons. Records on arrests and criminal charges of immigrants are not made available.[11] In this section, we focus on prison records to discuss the involvement of non-British citizens in criminal activities in the UK.

Prison statistics disaggregated by nationality are available for England and Wales. They are provided by the UK Ministry of Justice on a snapshot taken on the 30th of June of each year. Data are consistently reported from June 2002 to June 2016. We discuss these prison records in this section.

Numbers. In 2016, the overall UK prison population comprised almost 95,000 individuals. The majority of them – 85,100 (89%) – were detained in England. Prisons located in Scotland and

---

[11] Arrest data by nationality, for some years and some areas of the UK, are discussed in Bell et al. (2013).

Wales hosted 7,700 (8%) and 1,800 (1.9%) inmates, respectively.[12] Figure 3.6 illustrates that the number of British inmates steadily increased from 62,500 in 2002 to 74,900 in 2016, a 20% increase over fifteen years. Throughout the period, they accounted for 85% to 88% of the detained population. The population of foreign nationals in prison showed a different trend: they quickly expanded between 2002 and 2008, increasing from 7,700 to 11,400, and then started to gradually decline in the following years. At the end of June 2016, there were approximately 9.9 foreign born inmates in England and Wales, accounting for 11.6% of the total prison population.[13] The continuous line in Figure 3.6 reports foreign nationals as a share of the total prison population. This share started at 10.8% in 2002, peaked at 14% in 2006, and then gradually declined to 11.6% in 2016, following the downward trend in foreign inmates and the upward trend in British ones.

The dashed black line in Figure 3.6 reports the share of foreign nationals over the total resident population that we discussed in Figure 3.2. As explained in Section 3.2.2, the actual size of the immigrant population in the UK is better captured by counting foreign-born individuals rather than foreign nationals. Prison records, however, identify immigrants through nationality rather than country of birth: in this section, we adopt their definition to ensure comparability of immigrant shares. The comparison between the two lines in Figure 3.6 provides a visual answer to the question regarding the over- rather than under-representation of immigrants in UK prisons. Between 2002 and 2016, the share of foreign nationals over the prison population is systematically above the share over the total resident population. The gap is fairly large at the beginning of the period: in 2002, non-British citizens accounted for 4.5% of the

---

[12]   As for reported crime, we discuss only statistics for England and Wales.

[13]   A residual category, 'Nationality Not Recorded', accounts for 0.5% to 1% of the prison population in all years. Note that information on nationality (as well as ethnicity and religion) is obtained from self-reports of prisoners and it is not checked by prison establishments before being entered in the statistical database.

population residing in the UK and 10.8% of its prison population. This corresponds to an over-representation by a factor of about 2.4. The steady expansion in the population of foreign nationals in the UK, contrasted with the relatively flat presence of foreign nationals in UK prisons, led to a gradual narrowing of this gap. In 2015, foreign citizens were 8.6% of the resident population and 12.2% of the prison population: they were still over-represented in prison, but the factor declined to 1.4.

Detention status. The British prison population is classified into three categories (UK Ministry of Justice, 2016): (1) sentenced: those held in custody as a result of receiving a sentence in a criminal court; (2) on remand: those awaiting commencement or continuation of trial prior to verdict; (3) non-criminal prisoners: individuals held for civil offences (e.g. non-payment of council tax or contempt of court) or under the Immigration Act; the non-criminal population also includes immigration detainees who have finished serving their a criminal sentence and are being kept in prison by immigration authorities, and those detained in Immigration Removal Centres (IRCs) pending their extradition or deportation.[14]

Figure 3.7 shows the status of British and foreign national detainees in 2002, 2009, and 2016. In 2002, more than 80% of British inmates were 'sentenced' and this share increased to almost 90% in 2016. At the same time, the share of those on remand declined from 18% to 10%, while the number of non-criminal prisoners among natives was close to zero throughout the entire period. Figures and trends are distinctively different for foreign nationals. The share of detained immigrants with a conviction is always lower than that of natives and declining over time: it was 73% in 2002 and declined to 68% in 2016. Those on remand are fairly stable at around 20%, while a substantial and increasing share of foreign nationals in detention are

[14]   A fourth category is 'Recalls', those held in custody for breaching the terms of their licence conditions following release into the community. These detainees are counted as a subcategory of those sentenced.

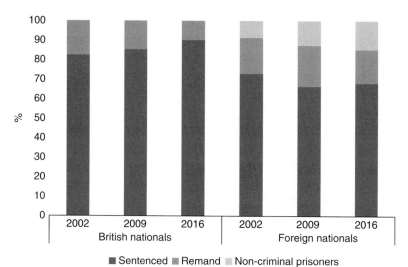

FIGURE 3.7 British and foreign nationals detained, by status, 2002, 2009, and 2016.

Source: Authors' calculations based on Ministry of Justice data.

classified as 'non-criminal prisoners'. This latter share increased from 9% in 2002 to 15% in 2016. This increase can be partially explained by the intense creation of immigration-related crimes that occurred in the UK during that same time period. Aliverti (2013) counts eighty-four new criminal and civil offences in immigration law introduced since 1999, in what she defines 'the fastest and largest expansion of immigration crimes since 1905' (p. 3). Immigration crimes do not refer to ordinary offences such as theft or burglary committed by immigrants. Rather, they are breaches to immigration legislation – e.g. illegal entry, obtaining leave to remain in the UK by deception, employing someone who does not have legal permission to work, etc. – and can be committed by both British citizens and non-citizens.

Sentence duration. Prison records also allow us to compare the distributions of sentences handed down to UK natives and foreign-born nationals. As displayed in Figure 3.8, the two distributions in June 2016 were very similar to each other. Immigrants are only slightly more likely to have very short sentences than natives:

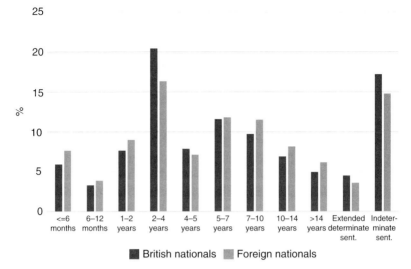

FIGURE 3.8 Prison population by sentence length: British and foreign nationals, 2016.

Source: Authors' calculations based on Ministry of Justice data.

20.5% of foreign detainees (with a final conviction) had a sentence length lower than two years versus 16.8% among natives. This gap vanishes when considering sentences shorter than four years, for which the share of inmates is 36.8% for immigrants and 37.3% for UK citizens. Similarly, the share of criminals sentenced to less than ten years of imprisonment is almost identical across the two groups: 67.3% for foreign nationals and 66.4% for immigrants. There was also hardly any difference in sentence lengths for very serious offenders: roughly 20% of inmates in both groups were sentenced to more than fourteen years of prison, or received an extended determinate or indeterminate sentence.[15]

---

[15]   'Extended determinate sentences' are given to provide extra protection to the public in certain types of cases in which the court has found that the offender is dangerous and extra precautions are required to protect the public from risk of harm. An 'indeterminate prison sentence' is usually given for the most serious crimes if the judge believes that the offender poses a threat to the public and usually contain a minimum term, known as a tariff, which the prisoner must serve before being considered for release. The actual date of release is decided by the independent Parole Board. See UK Ministry of Justice (2016).

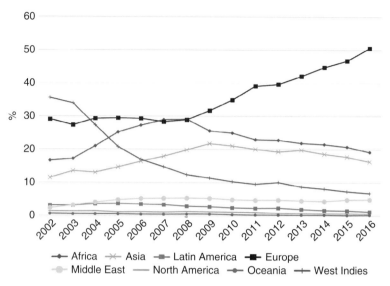

FIGURE 3.9 Foreign national detainees, share by area of origin, 2002–16.
Source: Authors' calculations based on Ministry of Justice data.

Removals of foreign national offenders. The British government has been fairly effective in removing foreign national offenders in recent years. Between 2007 and 2014, almost 40,000 offenders were deported back to their origin country after being convicted or having served their sentence in the UK prison system (National Audit Office, 2014). The number of offenders removed has remained fairly constant over this time period, at approximately 5,000 every year.

Nationalities. Figure 3.9 disaggregates foreign national detainees by area of origin from 2002 to 2016. The nationality composition of the immigrant prison population changed quite dramatically over this span of time. As expected, some of these changes resemble the evolution in the origin composition of immigrant inflows to the UK that we discussed in Section 3.2.3. In 2002, the largest group of foreign inmates was from West Indies (35.5%), followed by Europe (29%), Africa (16.7%), Asia (11.4%), Latin American (3.1%), Middle East (2.3%), North America (1.6%), and Oceania (0.4%). In 2016, Europeans

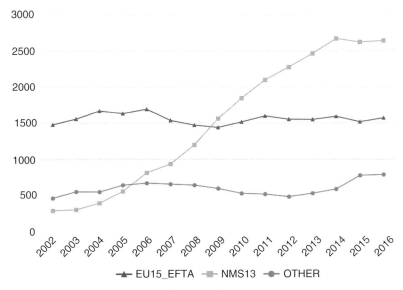

FIGURE 3.10 European detainees, by macro-area, 2002–16.
Source: Authors' calculations based on Ministry of Justice data.

accounted for slightly more than half of the immigrant inmates
(50.5%); Africans were in second place (19.2%), followed by Asians
(16.4%), while West Indies dropped to the fourth place (6.8%), just
above citizens from the Middle East (4.9%). The remaining areas of
origin (Latin America, North America, and Oceania) together
accounted for fewer than 2.5%.

Table A.2 shows that detainees from the Middle East experienced the largest increase in percentage terms (+170%) between 2002
and 2016, rising from 179 to 484. A similarly sizeable jump is recorded
for Europeans, an increase from 2,239 in 2002 to 4,999 in 2016
(+123%). Asians and Africans were also on the rise (+83% and +48%,
respectively), while all other national groups declined. The share of
West Indians among incarcerated immigrants, in particular, dropped
by 75% over this period.

Figure 3.10 takes a closer look at Europeans, showing that the
increase in European detainees from 2002 to 2016 is almost entirely
driven by citizens of the thirteen NMS (Bulgaria, Croatia, Cyprus,

Czech Republic, Estonia, Hungary, Latvia, Lithuania, Malta, Poland, Romania, Slovakia, and Slovenia) that joined the EU between 2004 and 2013. Inmates from NMS13, indeed, increased from 295 in 2002 to 2,640 in 2016 and became the largest group in 2009, exceeding EU15 citizens, plus Iceland, Lichtenstein, Norway, and Switzerland (EFTA – European Free Trade Association), who had been the leading group until then. In sharp contrast to the upward trend in NMS13 citizens, EU15 + EFTA and Other Europeans remained fairly flat over the entire period we observe.

Table A.3 contrasts the ranking of the ten main nationalities of European citizens detained in British prisons in 2002 with the corresponding ranking in 2016. The arrival of immigrants from NMS after 2004 is clearly visible in the differences in nationality mix between the two periods. In 2002, Irish Republic nationals accounted for 30% of the European detainees, followed by Turkey (10%); the Netherlands (9%); Spain, Serbia, and Italy (all at 5%); Germany, France, and Portugal (all at 4%); and, finally, Albania (3%). In 2016, instead, the ranking is the following: Poland (20%), Irish Republic (15%), Romania (13%), Albania (10%), Lithuania (9%), Portugal (5%), the Netherlands and Latvia (both at 3%), and Italy and Slovakia (both at 2%).

3.5 DO IMMIGRANTS CAUSE CRIME IN THE UK?

This section addresses the important policy question of whether the presence of immigrants in an area leads to higher local crime rates in the UK. We first review previous studies on the British context (Section 3.5.1) and we then provide new empirical evidence on this issue (Section 3.5.2).

3.5.1 Previous Research

Bell et al. (2013) estimate longitudinal regression of recorded crime rates on local immigrant population in England and Wales over the period 2001–08. They examine the impact on violent and property crime of two large immigrant flows that occurred over that period. The first wave was caused by the eruption and intensification of conflicts in many countries – such as Iraq, Afghanistan, Somalia, and the former Yugoslavia – that led to a dramatic increase in asylum seekers during the late 1990s and early 2000s. The second inflow was determined by the expansion of the European Union in 2004 to include the so-called A8 countries (Poland, Hungary, Czech Republic, Slovakia, Slovenia, Estonia, Latvia, and Lithuania) and by the decision of the UK to allow immediate and unrestricted labour market access to citizens from these NMS (see Section 3.2.1). Bell et al. (2013) deal with the potential endogeneity of migrants' residential choices using an instrumental variable (IV) approach. For the population of asylum seekers, they use a dispersal policy adopted by the British government in 2001. From that date, asylum applicants were dispersed to locations around the UK while their status was being determined. The choice of locations was made by the National Asylum Support Service (NASS) without taking into consideration applicants' desires and requests. This dispersal policy can thus be used as an instrument for the location of asylum seekers across British local authorities under the identifying assumption that locations were not chosen in response to crime shocks. A8 immigrants were instead allowed to freely choose where to settle in the UK. In their case, Bell et al. (2013) relied on the well-established empirical fact that prior settlement patterns of migrants from the same national/ethnic group have a strong predictive effect of location choices of new arrivals from the same group (Bartel, 1989). Following Altonji and Card (1991), they constructed a so-called 'supply-push component' instrument. This empirical strategy – widely used in the economic literature that studies migration impact on different host country outcomes – is used and explained in detail in the next section.

According to the findings in Bell et al. (2013), the very rapid influx of A8 migrants who entered the UK after the EU enlargement in 2004 had no detrimental crime impact. On the contrary, they identify a crime-reduction effect of A8 citizens on property crime. The results for the asylum seeker wave, instead, point at an increase in property crime in areas that were assigned more asylum seekers. Their estimates imply that a 1 percentage point increase in the share of asylum seekers in the local population is associated with a rise of 0.93% in property crimes, while a similar rise in A8 migrants reduces property crime by 0.29%. In both cases, the effect is statistically significant, although quantitatively small.

The authors interpret these findings within a standard economic model of criminal behaviour. While A8 immigrants were allowed to choose locations that offered the best labour market opportunities for their skills, asylum seekers were placed in economically depressed areas and legally prevented from having a formal employment for the first six months after filing their asylum application. Weaker economic integration – clearly highlighted by the large employment gap between the two groups – likely provided more incentives to engage in crime to asylum applicants than A8 immigrants.

In a related paper, Bell and Machin (2013) focus on the relation between immigrants' enclaves and crime. Using both recorded crime and self-reported crime victimization data, they show that crime (violent crime in particular) is substantially lower in enclaves, that is, in neighbourhoods where the immigrant population share is particularly high. They show that this crime-reduction effect is present for both natives and immigrants living in such neighbourhoods. To explain this beneficial 'enclave effect' they discuss the role of sorting and of social interactions in shaping the immigration–crime link.

Jaitman and Machin (2013) estimate spatial panel data models of the crime–immigration relationship in England and Wales over the 2000s, and present an analysis of differences in arrest rates of natives and migrants using unique data from the London Metropolitan Police Service. Similarly to Bell et al. (2013), they use a 'supply-push component' instrumental variable approach to address the endogeneity of immigrant population distribution across areas and over time. They find no evidence of an average causal impact of immigration on criminal behaviour. When considering A8 and non-A8 immigrants separately, they find no significant effect for any of the two groups. In their analysis of arrest data, they find no difference in the likelihood of being arrested between natives and immigrants.

3.5.2 New Evidence

In this section, we use the latest available data and provide novel evidence on the impact of immigrant population on crime rate in the UK. As we discuss in the text that follows, our estimates broadly confirm the findings we described in the previous section. As a matter of fact, areas in the UK that received stronger inflows of immigrants in recent years did not seem to have experienced larger increases in crime rate than areas whose foreign population remained constant or declined.

3.5.2.1 Data

To perform our empirical analysis, we constructed a longitudinal dataset of Local Authorities (LAs) of England and Wales with annual observations on crime rates, immigrant population, and other local controls. The data span eleven years, from 2004 to 2014. We managed to include 315 LAs in our sample: 272 LAs have valid records for the entire period we consider, while the remaining 43 have some missing values in some years between 2004 and 2016. In particular, estimates of the immigrant population at the LA level are not available for LAs that host very small numbers of immigrants. Our final dataset is an unbalanced panel that contains 3,018 observations.[16]

Crime data are provided by the Home Office and recorded over the twelve months from the 1st of April of one year to the 31st of March of the following year. In our analysis, crimes committed in year y include all crimes committed between the 1st of April of year y to the 31st of March of year $y + 1$. Data on immigrant populations (foreign-born and foreign nationals) are obtained from ONS, as well as data on the other local controls (population, employment rate, share of males aged 16 to 24).

[16] Our estimates are basically identical when restricting the sample to the balanced panel of 272 LAs.

3.5.2.2 Descriptive Statistics

Descriptive statistics for the main variables used in our empirical analysis are reported in Table A.4. The outcome variables we will try to explain with immigration rates and policies are local authority crime rates, measured as number of yearly offences per 10,000 population. Offences are grouped into four broad categories: property, violent, drug, and other crime. Property crimes are the most frequent type of offences: in average, there are 507.7 offences (per 10,000 population) per year in each LA. Over the period covered in our sample, the lowest property crime rate was 141.1 crimes per 10,000 people and the highest 2,298.7 crimes per 10,000 people, with a standard deviation equal to 219.9. The average violent crime rate is 147.4 crimes per 10,000 people and its standard deviation is 66.5 (the lowest crime rate recorded in our sample is 36 and the highest is 452.2 crimes per 10,000 people. Average drug and other crime rate are substantially lower, 34.5 crimes per 10,000 people and 39.4 crimes per 10,000 people, respectively. In our sample, property crime accounts for almost 70% of all recorded offences, violent offences for 20%, and drug crime and other crime for 5% each.

The average share of the population that is foreign born is 10.5%, which ranges from 0.8% in the semirural district of Amber Valley (in 2012) in the East Midlands to 58% in the London Borough of Brent (in 2011). Its standard deviation is 10.1. The average share of foreign nationals is equal to 6.8% in our sample, with a standard deviation of 6.7.

Finally, Table A.4 shows that the average local authority has a population of approximately 166,000 inhabitants, an employment rate equal to 72.5% and a share of males aged 16 to 24 (over total population) of about 5.7%.

3.5.2.3 Graphical Evidence

We start our analysis by providing some graphical evidence on the relation between local crime and the presence of immigrants in the area. If immigrants led to higher crime rates, we should possibly

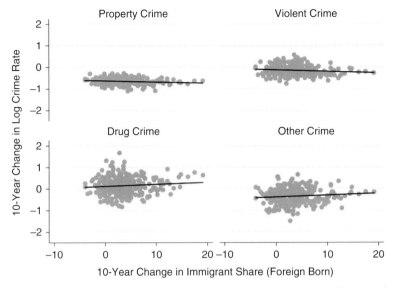

FIGURE 3.11 Log crime rate and immigrant share: ten-year (2004–14) changes, by type of offence.

Note: The figure displays the scatterplot of ten-year changes in log crime rate (vertical axis) versus ten-year changes in immigrant share (measured with foreign-born population). Each dot corresponds to a Local Authority in England and Wales. Each subgraph refers to a different type of crime. The differences are computed between 2014 and 2004.

Source: Authors' calculations based on UK Office for National Statistics and Home Office data.

observe that areas that received larger inflows of immigrants experienced larger increases in the number of committed offences.

Figure 3.11 reports the scatterplot of ten-year changes in log crime rates (on the vertical axis) against ten-year changes in the share of foreign-born over total population (on the horizontal axis). These long-run differences are computed between 2014 and 2004 – covering the entire period we study in our regression analysis – and each dot in the figure corresponds to a different LA. A different macro-group of offences – property, violent, drug, and other crime – is displayed in each of the four subgraphs. Figure 3.11 shows an unambiguously flat slope for both property and violent crime and a slightly

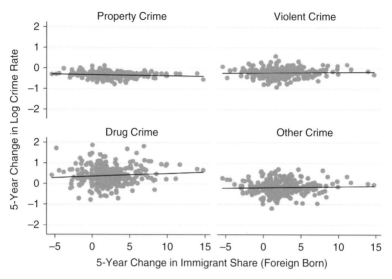

FIGURE 3.12 Log crime rate and immigrant share: five-year (2004–09) changes, by type of offence.

Note: The figure displays the scatterplot of five-year changes in log crime rate (vertical axis) versus five-year changes in immigrant share (measured with foreign-born population). Each dot corresponds to a Local Authority in England and Wales. Each subgraph refers to a different type of crime. The differences are computed between 2004 and 2009.

Source: Authors' calculations based on UK Office for National Statistics and Home Office data.

positive one for drug and other crime. Overall, the graph points at the absence of any strong long-run correlation between hosting more immigrants and having higher crime rates.

In Figures 3.12 and 3.13, we split the period of observation in two sub-periods (2004–09 and 2009–14) and we take medium-run differences over five years. This symmetric split of our sample roughly corresponds with a pre– and post–Great Recession division of our data. Insofar as worse labour market conditions may induce immigrants to engage more in crime, a larger immigrant population may imply more crime during an economic downturn while having no effect in good times. Figure 3.12 refers to the 2004–09 period: the fitted line is flat for property, violent, and other crime, and only slightly positive for drug crime. Overall, these medium-run differences also point to the absence of an

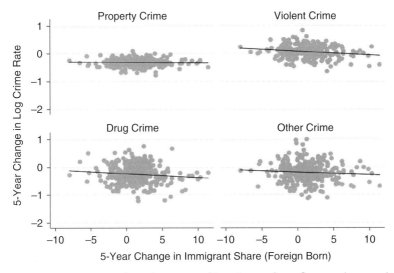

FIGURE 3.13 Log crime rate and immigrant share: five-year (2009–14) changes, by type of offence.

Note: The figure displays the scatterplot of five-year changes in log crime rate (vertical axis) versus five-year changes in immigrant share (measured with foreign-born population). Each dot corresponds to a Local Authority in England and Wales. Each subgraph refers to a different type of crime. The differences are computed between 2009 and 2014.

Source: Authors' calculations based on UK Office for National Statistics and Home Office data.

obvious quantitative relation between immigration and crime. A similar picture emerges from Figure 3.13: even when considering the years immediately following the economic downturn caused by the 2007–08 global financial crisis, we fail to observe that areas that received larger inflows of foreign-born citizens suffered larger increases in local crime rates. In the following two sections, we empirically investigate the conjecture that the crime–immigration link may have changed during the Great Recession.

3.5.2.4 *Empirical Strategy*

We now estimate spatial panel data models of crime and immigration population, in which LAs are the geographical unit of analysis. We estimate first-differences equations. This means that we examine how yearly changes in the immigrant population residing in one area impact on yearly changes in local crime rates, controlling for changes in other variables that may also influence crime. We estimate the following regression equation:

$$\Delta \ln\left(\frac{\text{crime}_{rt}}{\text{pop}_{rt}}\right) = \beta\Delta\left(\frac{\text{imm}_{rt}}{\text{pop}_{rt}}\right) + \gamma\Delta X_{rt} + \theta_t + \varepsilon_{rt} \qquad (3.1)$$

where $\ln\left(\frac{\text{crime}_{rt}}{\text{pop}_{rt}}\right)$ is the log crime rate (number of offences per 10,000 population) recorded in area r in year t; $\left(\frac{\text{imm}_{rt}}{\text{pop}_{rt}}\right)$ is the number of immigrants residing in area r in year t relative to that area's total population; X_{rt} is a vector of local area controls that are gradually added in our specification: log total population, employment rate, share of males aged 16 to 24; θ_t are year dummies that capture any national-level variation in immigration and crime; and ε_{rt} is an idiosyncratic shock. The Δ operator means that, for each variable, we are taking the difference between the values in the current year (t) and in the previous year $(t-1)$.[17]

An obvious concern in estimating this equation is the potential endogeneity of the residential locations of immigrants. More economically deprived areas, for instance, generally have higher crime rates: higher exposure to victimization risk tends to exert downward pressure on housing prices (Gibbons, 2004; Pope, 2008) and, in turn, more affordable housing may attract more immigrants. In the data, we may then observe that high crime areas have a larger population of foreign-born residents, even in the absence of a causal impact of the latter variable on the former. By using a first-differences estimator we can disregard any such worry about time-invariant area characteristics that may drive both the size of the foreign population and the level

---

[17]   In some specifications, we also include dummies for each of the forty-three police force areas (PFAs) that, in a first-difference model, controls for area-specific time trends. All decisions on police staffing and enforcement priorities are determined at the PFA level, meaning that the inclusion of PFA dummies allows for linear variation over time in the effect produced by systematic differences in those decisions on crime rates.

of crime. Indeed, we do not compare areas (e.g. wealthy vs. deprived areas) but rather we analyse variation within areas and over time. In other words, we look, for instance, at a deprived area, and we test whether increases in the foreign-born resident population are associated with increases in local crime rates. Our estimates, however, may still be biased by time-varying shocks that cause changes in both crime rates and local immigrant numbers. For example, if immigrants decide to locate in areas experiencing low (or negative) crime growth, this would generate a downward bias in our estimates. Vice versa, if they move into areas with increasing crime rates, the bias would go in the opposite direction. A priori, it is difficult to say how migrants' residential decisions should react to such shocks. On the one hand, they should move into areas that are experiencing economic growth (and hence, possibly, low crime growth) because they offer better labour market prospects. On the other hand, they may prefer to reside in areas that are going through a local economic downturn in order to find cheaper accommodation.

We address this endogeneity concern by using an instrumental variable approach that is standard in the economics of migration literature. Following Altonji and Card (1991), spatial correlation analyses of the impact of migration on different host country outcomes have often used a so-called 'supply-push component' instrument. In studying the impact of immigrants on local crime rates, for instance, this instrumental variable approach has been adopted by both Bianchi et al. (2012) for Italy and Bell et al. (2013) for the UK. The rationale for this approach is based on the observed persistence of location choices of immigrants in host countries: immigrants tend to go where earlier cohorts have already established immigrant enclaves (Bartel, 1989). The instrument is constructed using an 'initial' distribution of immigrants across different areas and the current national inflow of new entrants by country/region of origin. The assumed conditional exogeneity of this instrumental variable with respect to local shocks follows from the fact that the first component is predetermined with respect to the period under study (and thus assumed to be uncorrelated with any shock occurring in that the actual study period) while the second component varies at the national level (and is therefore driven predominantly by shocks to source countries and changes in national policies in destination countries).

Our instrument SP_{rt} is defined as

$$SP_{rt} = \sum_a \overline{sh}_{ar91} * Imm_{at} \tag{3.2}$$

$\overline{sh}_{ar91}$ is the share of immigrants from macro-area a living in region r in year 1991. The data come from the full 100% sample of the 1991 British Census: the geographical unit of observation is a local authority and we have eight macro-areas of origin: (1) EU, (2) other European, (3) North America, (4) Latin America, (5) Africa, (6) Middle East, (7) rest of Asia, and (8) Oceania. Imm_{at} is the national net annual inflow of immigrants from each area of origin a in year t for the period 2003–14. Such inflows are measured as yearly changes in the foreign-born population residing in the UK, a number that is estimated using Annual Population Survey data. In our IV regressions, the variable SP_{rt} is used as an instrument for the contemporaneous immigrants share in the local authority.

3.5.2.5   Results

Main results. Table A.5 reports our main ordinary least squares (OLS)–based estimates of Eq. (3.1). Recall that, for reasons discussed in Section 3.2.2, the immigrant share in the local authority is measured using the foreign-born population. We exclusively report the estimated β coefficient, which is our estimate of the effect of the immigrant share in the area on local crime rates. Note that each reported coefficient comes from a separate regression with a different set of control variables. In column 1, we condition only on a full set of year dummies. We then gradually add the following local controls: log population (column 2), employment rate (column 3), and share of males aged 16 to 24 (column 5). Finally, in column 5, we condition on all observed variables along with a full set of forty-three Police Force dummy variables to capture any nuisance trends at the PFA level. We separately look at four categories of offences: property crime (panel A), violent crime (panel B), drug crime (panel C), and other crime (panel D). We maintain the same structure in all the following tables of regression results. In all regressions, standard errors are clustered at the LA level to allow for any within-LA serial correlation in shocks.

According to Table A.5, areas that received larger inflows of immigrants did not necessarily experience increases in local offending rate. Irrespective of the type of offence and specification, all estimated coefficients are qualitatively indistinguishable from zero and not statistically significant, suggesting the absence of a correlation between the two variables of interest.

Using foreign nationals. In Table A.6, we test the robustness of the previous findings to the use of an alternative measure of local immigrant population: we now define the local immigrant share using foreign nationals rather than foreign-born individuals. As discussed in Section 3.2.2, when immigrants are identified based on nationality rather than country of birth, the size of the immigrant population shrinks considerably. Estimates of the population of foreign nationals are available for a slightly smaller set of LA, leading to a reduction in our sample from 3,018 observations to 2,779. The estimated coefficients in Table A.6 are very similar to those reported in Table A.5. There is no significant correlation between changes in local crime rates and changes in the foreign national population who reside in the area for any of the four offences category we consider.

The Great Recession. In Table A.7, we investigate whether the relationship between crime and immigrant residents in the area changed with the arrival of the Great Recession. The economic slowdown that followed the financial crisis of 2007 resulted in a severe decline of UK gross domestic product (GDP) growth, with growth falling by over 6 percentage points between 2008 and 2009. The unemployment rate increased from just over 5% in the second quarter of 2008 to almost 8% by the second quarter of 2009 and then remained fairly constant around this level (peaking at 8.4% in the last quarter of 2011) until mid-2013, when it started declining and returned at about 5% in 2016.

Immigrants are often employed in low-skilled occupations, in jobs that are temporary or seasonal in nature, and have, on average, shorter job tenure than natives. These factors may strongly increase their likelihood to become unemployed during an economic downturn with respect to natives. Indeed, Dustmann et al. (2010) analysed British data from 1981 to 2005 and found larger unemployment responses to economic shocks for low-skilled workers relative to high-skilled workers, and for immigrants relative to natives within the same skill group. The obtained similar results for Germany.

Even if the negative employment effects of the 2008 recession were not differentially more severe for immigrants than for natives, we may wonder whether poorer labour market conditions induced migrants to engage more in crime. To address this question, we reestimate Eq. (3.1) but we now include an interaction term of the immigrant share with a dummy equal one after year 2008 (post2008). The estimating equation is

$$\Delta \ln \left(\frac{\text{crime}_{rt}}{\text{pop}_{rt}} \right) = \beta_1 \Delta \left(\frac{\text{imm}_{rt}}{\text{pop}_{rt}} \right) + \beta_2 \left[\Delta \left(\frac{\text{imm}_{rt}}{\text{pop}_{rt}} \right) * \text{post2008} \right]$$

$$+ \gamma \Delta X_{rt} + \theta_t + \varepsilon_{rt} \tag{3.3}$$

where the coefficient β_1 identifies the effect of changes in the local immigrant share on crime while the coefficient β_2 identifies the additional effect (if any) of changes in immigration in the aftermath of the 2008 global financial crisis. Results from estimating Eq. (3.3) are reported in Table A.7. The structure of the table follows Tables A.5 and A.6, but we now show both β_1 and β_2 coefficients.

Our findings for property and violent crime seem to support the conjecture that harsher economic conditions may lead to more offending behaviour by immigrants, or more specifically, dampen the general reduction in crime that is generally observed when the size of an immigrant population increases. In both panel A and panel B, the estimated coefficients β_1 and β_2 have opposite sign. For property crime, we find a negative and significant effect of changes in the local foreign-born population on the number of offences (first row of panel A), suggesting that a larger presence of immigrants is associated to a reduction in offences against properties in the areas where they lived. The estimated coefficient on the interaction term (second row of panel A) is equal in size to the previous one, and is also significant but has opposite sign, which implies that the possible crime-reducing effect of immigration vanished in the years after 2008. As far as violent crime is concerned, estimates in panel B show that immigrants did not generally alter the number of offences in an area, but during recession years there is a positive relationship between the fraction of the local population that is foreign born and the crime rate. Indeed, while the coefficients in the first row of panel B are not significant, the interaction term delivers a positive and significant estimate. A similar pattern is observed for 'other crime' in panel D: estimates imply that more immigrant residents are associated with an increase in offences belonging to this category exclusively in the years after 2008. Our estimates for drug crime, instead, point somewhat in the opposite direction. In panel C, the estimated β_1 coefficient is positive while β_2 is negative: more immigrants are associated with more drug offences on average, but the effect tends to disappear during a recession.

IV estimates. We conclude this section by reporting our estimates of the crime–immigration relationship in which the potentially endogenous changes in the local immigrant share are instrumented with the 'supply-push' component described in the previous section. If the OLS estimates presented so far may be potentially (upward or downward) biased by the endogenous residential decisions of immigrants in response to local authority shocks, the IV estimates should arguably better identify the causal effect of immigration on crime. These IV estimates are reported in Table A.8.

The last row reports the first-stage F-statistics of the excluded instrument; a 'rule of thumb' indicator of the strength of instrument is whether or not this F-statistic is larger than 10 (Staiger and Stock, 1997). By this metric, our proposed instrument is a reasonably strong predictor of the potentially endogenous changes in local immigrant share in most of the specifications (in columns 1–4, the F-statistic varies between 9 and 18). The instrument becomes particularly weak (the F-statistic is equal to 2.8) only when PFA dummies are included in the specification (column 5), suggesting particular caution is warranted in interpreting this last set of estimates. These caveats aside, IV estimates confirm our previous OLS findings. There is no significant effect on property crime. A negative and significant coefficient on violent crime in the first column becomes insignificant as soon as local controls are included in the specification. None of the estimated relationships between immigration and drug crime are statistically different from zero. The IV estimates suggest that there may be a positive effect of immigration on 'other crime', but the magnitude of this estimated effect is quantitatively small, and this residual category of crime only account for 5% of total recorded crime. We therefore conclude that there is hardly any empirical evidence that immigrants in the UK have caused an increase in local crime rates.

3.6   CONCLUSIONS

The UK has received substantial inflows of immigrants in recent years. Its foreign-born population more than doubled in the last fifteen years, growing from 4.4 million in 2000 to almost 9.4 million in 2017. As a share of the total resident population, immigrants grew from 8% to 14% over the same period. If immigrants have a higher propensity to engage in crime than natives, this dramatic expansion of the immigrant population should be reflected in a parallel rise in crime rates relative to what we might reasonably have expected. In this chapter, we have analysed different pieces of evidence to understand whether immigrants made UK a more dangerous place where to live. Overall, we find little evidence to support this claim.

A simple comparison between the steep upward trend in immigrant population over the last fifteen years and the strong decline in criminal offences recorded over the same period of time suggests that the immigration–crime link is weak at the aggregate level. In fact, the UK experienced a remarkable decline in crime rate while recording unprecedented levels of net immigration. Total offences, as estimated by Crime Survey for England and Wales, were 43% lower in 2014 than in 2002, while police-recorded offences dropped by 30% over the same period of time.

Prison statistics show that foreign nationals are over-represented in prison, but the degree of over-representation has declined over time. Further, the growing presence of immigrants in the UK more generally has not been accompanied by a similar growth in the foreign prison population. In June 2016, there were approximately 9,900 foreign-born inmates in England and Wales, accounting for 11.6% of the total prison population. The share was very similar in 2002, when it was 10.8% percent, and there were 7,700 foreign national inmates. In 2002, non-British citizens accounted for 4.5% of the population residing in the UK and 10.8% of its prison population. In 2015, foreign citizens were 8.6% of the resident population and 12.2% of the prison population: they were still over-represented in prison, but the factor declined from 2.4 to 1.4. Notably, a growing fraction of the foreign detainees are held in prison as 'non-criminal prisoners' because they breached immigration law, but they did not commit any criminal offence.

Finally, we addressed the empirical question of whether the presence of immigrants in an area leads to an increase in local crime rates. After reviewing previous research on the British context, we provided new empirical evidence on this issue. We estimated spatial panel data models of crime and immigration population in which the geographical unit of analysis are Local Authorities in England and Wales. We produced first differences estimates and developed an instrumental variable strategy to deal with the potential endogeneity in residential choices of immigrants. Our findings are in line with those in previous studies for the UK. Far from finding a clear increase in crime due to a higher presence for immigrants in the area, we generally found no significant effect and even some estimates that point in the opposite direction, suggesting that increases in immigration may be associated with neighbourhoods becoming more, not less, safe. In further results, we investigated whether the relationship between crime and immigrant residents in the area changed with the arrival of the Great Recession. We found evidence consistent with a standard economic model of crime whereby more offending is observed when economic conditions worsen.

4   The Case of the United States

According to the US Census Bureau, as of 1 July 2017, just over 98% of all people living in the USA are the descendants of immigrants.[1] Over the course of the country's 250-year history, the rate of immigration and the composition of immigrants have varied dramatically. In the years between 1910 and 2013, roughly 5% to 15% of the US population was born outside of the country, with peaks in 1910 and 2013 and troughs in the 1960s and 1970s. The first immigrants were primarily from Western Europe, followed by a steady stream of forced immigration from Africa as part of the international slave trade. Over time, the fraction of immigrants coming from Eastern Europe and Asia increased, along with immigrants from countries north and south of the US borders; the Pew Research Center estimates that between 1965 and 2013, roughly one-half of all US immigrants came from Latin America.

In this chapter, we discuss how the US federal government has responded to the waves of immigrants arriving at its borders, highlighting a consistent theme: a historical wariness of the 'otherness' of the new arrivals, focused on a perception that these new and different immigrants were more prone to crime and vice than those who arrived before. We point out that immigration policy has historically focused on preventing immigrants who have engaged in crime from entering in the first place, what we call 'ex ante' policies, but in the past 100 years

---

[1]   To be clear, the authors' acknowledge that, like in many countries colonized by Europeans, the term 'native' is commonly used in the USA to identify people of American Indian, Alaskan Native, or Native Hawaiian, rather than people of European, African, or Asian descent. In the interest of consistency with the other chapters in this book, we will use the term 'native' to refer to people born in the USA, or to naturalized citizens.

has increasingly used 'ex post' policies to alter the incentives of immigrants after they have arrived.

As we will show, available evidence on the actual crime rate of immigrants generally shows that these perceptions were based more on abstract fears than on actual behaviour. We also present new research documenting the effectiveness of ex ante policies, specifically the 1917 Literacy Act, in reducing the criminality of immigrants, and highlight recent research on the role of more modern ex post policies, specifically the Immigration Reform and Control Act of 1986, in changing the propensity of immigrants to commit and report crime.

4.1   INSTITUTIONAL BACKGROUND

Debate over US immigration policy has always been, at least implicitly, tied to concerns about the morality and social behaviour of immigrants. When faced with the spectre of an immigrant 'other' threatening to destabilize American society, federal immigration policy has attempted to manipulate the flow and composition of newcomers in two different ways: ex ante prohibitions on groups of people who were deemed threats to the tranquillity of American life, and ex post domestic policy changes that reduced the expected return to immigration with the dual aim of making the USA a less attractive destination while sheltering natives from any adverse wage and employment shocks. For most of US history, the former policy lever was used more frequently (although not exclusively), and historians commonly identify four distinct periods of US immigration policy based on the stringency of ex ante prohibitions in place: an 'Open Door' era from 1776 to 1880 when, with a few exceptions, the predominate federal immigration policies encouraged new arrivals; a 'Door Ajar' era from 1880 to 1920, where increasing nationality and human capital-based restrictions prevented certain groups of people from entering; a highly restrictive 'Pet Door' era from 1920 to 1950; and a 'Dutch Door' era from 1950 to the present, which relaxed national quotas in favour of policies encouraging family reunification and high-skilled immigration (Meyers, 2004). Unlike more broad reviews of US immigration policy (e.g. Abramitzky and Boustan, 2017), we will focus on how immigration policies have both responded to, and shaped, immigrant crime. When possible, we will use Census data on nationality and incarceration rates to differentiate between real and perceived changes in the criminal behaviour of the foreign-born population.

4.1.1 The Open Door: 1776–1880

Prior to the ratification of the US Constitution, the US federal government had minimal authority. Like most other governmental functions, immigration policy was essentially left to the states, and state governments interested in increasing their land values (and thus property tax receipts) tended to adopt policies that encouraged population growth. Consistent with this idea of encouraging entry, immigration policies enacted during this period were ex post behavioural regulations, enacted in response to concerns about the potentially subversive or otherwise dangerous activities by immigrants once they had established residency.

The first federal rule governing the citizenship process was the Naturalization Act of 1790, plausibly in response to concerns about radical French agents (Meyers, 2004). Under these new rules, any free white person who had lived in the USA for two years or more could apply for citizenship in a state court, as long as he or she had lived in that state for at least one year. If the court determined that the applicant was 'of good character' and swore an oath of allegiance to the USA, citizenship was granted to both the applicant and any of the applicant's children under the age of 21. Of course, citizenship was available only to 'white' people of Western European or Scandinavian ancestry, which could plausibly be argued to be an ex ante restriction.

Over the next decade, the amount of time that an immigrant was required to wait to become a citizen was gradually extended. The Naturalization Act of 1795 strengthened existing ex post restrictions, mandating a three-year waiting period between when someone declared his or her intent to become a citizen in a court and the person's actual admission to citizenship. The 1795 Act also placed restrictions on the ability of foreign-born people to move within the country; prior to declaring their intent to become a citizen, immigrants had to have lived in the USA for at least two years and the particular state of admission for at least one year. The time span over which they were required to demonstrate 'moral character' was made explicit; during the five years of living in the USA as an alien, he must prove that 'he has behaved as a man of a good moral character, attached to the principles of the constitution of the United States, and well-disposed to the good order and happiness of the same'. In 1789, the Alien and Sedition Acts added two additional years to the amount of time someone had to live in the USA before declaring his or her intent to become a citizen, and then required an additional nine years of residency before citizenship was granted.

There is a general consensus among most historians that this extended waiting period was aimed primarily at solidifying political power for the Federalist Party, which was more popular among groups who had been in the country for multiple generations, but stated arguments for the 1789 Alien Acts played to fears of the criminal immigrant that are familiar in tone, if not in target, to more modern fears: just outside US borders were 'hordes of Wild Irishmen ... the turbulent and disorderly of all the world [who come to the United States in order to] distract our tranquillity' (Massachusetts Representative Harrison Gray Otis, 1797). The longer waiting period addressed this problem by increasing the amount of time new arrivals were formally under surveillance by government officials, thus deterring immigrants from offending. Notably, to the extent that these rules were enforced, and any criminal or amoral behaviour recorded, it is unlikely that the new citizen would offend in the future; modern research suggests that someone who has committed a crime but not reoffended for seven years, substantially shorter than the mandated waiting period, is statistically no more likely to offend than an otherwise similar person who has never committed a crime (Blumstein and Nakamura, 2009).

After the Democratic Republicans gained control of the presidency from the Federalists, the 1789 Alien Acts were repealed by the Nationalization Act of 1802, and the former 1795-era waiting period was re-enacted. The 1802 Act also clarified that any court could approve citizenship, and that court would receive a total of one dollar for each family formally registered as new citizens.

The first expansion of citizenship to non-Europeans occurred in 1870, when people of African descent (i.e. former slaves) were allowed to apply for citizenship. The removal of the 'white' requirement for citizenship was pushed by Massachusetts Senator Charles Sumner, one of the most high-profile abolitionists, in order to elevate the status of black men and help protect potential Republican voters from the Ku Klux Klan in the South (Wang, 1997). Sumner also encouraged moving the power to grant citizenship from state to federal courts, but this amendment was defeated by representatives from rural western states who wanted to continue to encourage population growth (Wang, 1997). The addition of 'persons born in the Chinese empire' to the list of people eligible to apply for citizenship was debated at this time, but quickly shut down (Wang, 1997).

4.1.2 The Door Ajar: 1880–1920

Anti-Chinese sentiment was explicitly codified by the Chinese Exclusion Act of 1882, which prohibited immigration from China until 1892, and issued deportation orders for all Chinese people who had entered the country after 17 November 1880. The concerns about Chinese immigration were undoubtedly an attempt to reinforce the political and social power of the status quo; Chinese immigrants, typically single men who sent a significant fraction of their wages to family members in China, are believed to have placed strong downward pressure on wages and working conditions in western states (Gold, 2011). The public debate, however, focused on criminality and character, just as it had a century before when Irish people were the

Table 4.1 *Incarceration rates*

Age		1870 (%)	1880 (%)	1900 (%)	1910 (%)
		Census year			
16–25	Asian men	0	0.91	0.1	0
	Native men	0.30	0.50	0.50	0.47
26–35	Asian men	0	0.50	0.71	0.14
	Native men	0.28	0.51	0.49	0.50
36–45	Asian men	0	1.23	0.52	0.15
	Native men	0.12	0.27	0.29	0.32

unnerving 'others'. Chinese immigrants were 'morally the most debased people on the face of the earth' (Connecticut Senator Orville Platt, 1882), who 'bring every character of vice … [and would be] injurious in every sense of the word' (Texas Senator Samuel Bell Maxey, 1882). Much like the modern warnings about Mexican men with 'calves the size of cantaloupes because they've been hauling 75 pounds of marijuana across the desert' (Iowa Representative Steve King, 2013), Chinese men were linked to drug use, specifically opium, and all female Chinese immigrants were essentially assumed to be prostitutes (Gold, 2011).

Were fears of Asian criminals justified by data available at the time? Table 4.1 displays the relative incarceration rates for men living in the USA, based on their age, and whether or not they were born in the USA or in Asia, in 1870, 1880, 1900, and 1910. There were no people of Asian descent in correctional facilities in the 1870 Census. In 1880, right before the 1882 Exclusion Act was enacted, Asian men in their 'peak' crime years were incarcerated at almost twice the rate of natives, but 26- to 35-year-olds were in prison at essentially the same rate. In 1900, people at the peak of their criminal potential were much less likely to be incarcerated than similarly aged natives, but older Asians were more likely to be incarcerated than older natives. By 1910 Asian men were less likely to be incarcerated than natives across all age groups.

On its face, Census data suggest that late-nineteenth-century fears of Asian criminals may have been justified. However, many factors make a comparison of these raw numbers somewhat unreliable. Most importantly, Asian immigrants were only 1.6% the immigrant population of the USA in the 1880 Census, but were as much as 10% of the total population in western states such as California and Nevada. As states vary in both their criminal environment and propensity to use incarceration, it is possible that some of the difference between the incarceration rates for the Asian- and US-born could be due to differences in where they live. We therefore constructed an alternate 'weighted' native incarceration rate that places more emphasis on the incarceration rates for natives in California, and heavily discounts incarceration rates for natives in Pennsylvania and Illinois, where not many Asian-born people lived.[2]

As Figure 4.1 makes clear, the concentration of young Asian immigrants on the West Coast dramatically overstated the Asian incarceration rate relative to natives, particularly in 1880. Between 1870 and 1910, the incarceration rate of Asian people under 35 was indistinguishable, or lower, than that of natives. In contrast, older Asian men in 1880 were incarcerated at a rate that was almost three times that of older natives living in similar places. While this high rate is striking, it is difficult to square heighted criminal activity in the one (relatively small) group with a blanket prohibition on entire nations of people.

Concerns about the underlying criminal potential of immigrants were explicitly addressed for the first time in the Immigration Act of 1882, which banned people with criminal histories from

---

[2] To calculate the counterfactual incarceration rate for natives, we construct an age- and state-specific immigration weight, IW_{as}, that is equivalent to the percent of all immigrants in age group a who live in state s. We then calculate the native incarceration rate as

$$\text{Incarceration Rate}_a = \frac{\sum_s IW_{as} \times \text{Natives in Institutions}_{as}}{\sum_s IW_{as} \times \text{Natives}_{as}}$$

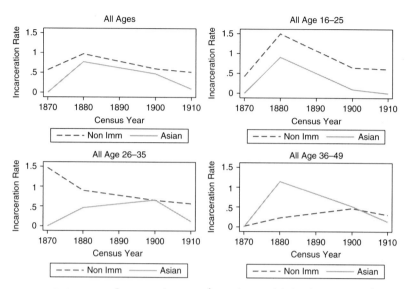

FIGURE 4.1 Incarceration rates for natives and Asian immigrants, by age group, 1870–1910.

entering the USA. This 1882 act also imposed a soft income test; individuals had to pay 50 cents (roughly $12 in 2015) as a processing fee, and also excluded people likely to become public charges (specifically the mentally ill or disabled). A medical exam was added to the requirements for entry in 1891, as well as a prohibition on 'paupers'.

The late 1800s also brought laws that restricted economic opportunities for immigrants, both ex post and ex ante. The Alien Contract Labor Law (ACLL) of 1885 prohibited American firms from hiring workers who were not currently residing in the USA (note the stark differences between this and the Italian 'click day' system). Two years later, the Payson Acts prohibited non-citizens from owning property, and amendments to the ACLL granted federal agents (eventually the US Treasury agents specifically) the right to inspect all ships prior to docking; the owner of the ship was responsible for transporting anyone who already had a job in the USA back to their country of origin. Exceptions were made for 'creative classes' – artists, singers, lecturers, or actors, and also for domestic servants. Advertising US employment opportunities in foreign cities was prohibited in 1891, and in 1903 the ACLL was amended to make even an 'implied' job opportunity criminal, unless the potential employer could demonstrate that there were no unemployed people in America who could perform the tasks necessary for the position. Exceptions to the ACLL were carved out for the right kind of immigrant, however; in 1903 the law was finally clarified to allow for 'persons belonging to any recognized learned profession'.

Taken together, the ACLL essentially increased the risk associated with travelling to America. Employment could no longer be secured prior to entry, and information about job availability in the USA was restricted to informal channels, rather than to public advertisements. As a result, one might expect that some potential immigrants would be deterred from attempting to enter the country. However, the impact that these laws would have on the decision to immigrate is not independent of someone's underlying propensity to commit crime, resulting in the ACLL potentially having the perverse effect of increasing the criminal behaviour of immigrants.

The logic of this effect is intuitive; suppose there are two types of potential immigrants: people who will move to a new country only if they know they will have a secure job and their own home, and people who are willing to take a risk in a new place. If immigrants are allowed to buy property and US employers are allowed to advertise open positions, then both types of people may choose to immigrate. Banning those advertisements, on the other hand, and forcing immigrants to rent, means that only risk seekers will choose to move. There is a long-standing, robust literature in criminology documenting a positive relationship between tolerance for risk and criminal activity (see, e.g. Farrington, 1998). This link may be biological; young children with slow heart rates and high arousal thresholds (sometimes known as 'stimulation seekers') are more likely to commit crimes even as adults (Moffitt et al., 2011). If all immigrants are risk seekers, owing to restrictions on legal hiring practices, we would expect a larger fraction of them would eventually engage in crime.

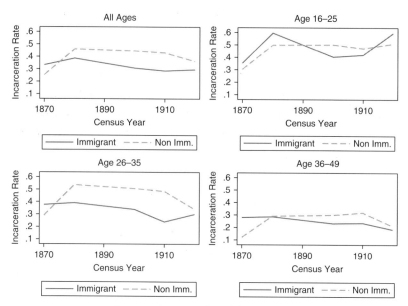

FIGURE 4.2 Incarceration rates (in %) for natives and immigrants, by age group, 1870–1920.

Did the combined effects of the ACLL and Immigration Act of 1882 make immigrants more criminal? The ban on people with active criminal records should have resulted in a downward shift in the propensity of immigrants to commit crime between 1880 and 1900, followed by an increase in criminality between 1900 and 1910, as the ACLL prohibitions were tightened.

Incarceration rates for natives and non-natives, displayed in Figure 4.2, are generally consistent with the hypothesis that the ex ante prohibitions on criminals lead to a reduction in immigrant crime, particularly among men under the age of 25, whose overall incarceration rates clearly fell more than those of natives between 1880 and 1900. The ex post restrictions, however, may not have changed the criminality of immigrants on average; there is little evidence of an increase in the relatively criminality of immigrant men between 1900 and 1910 – if anything, crime rates for men between 26 and 35 fell by more than those for natives.

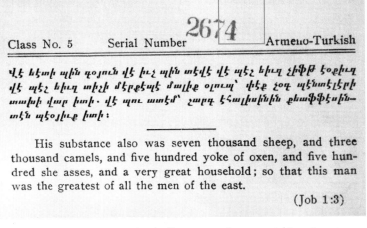

FIGURE 4.3 Example of a literacy test for potential immigrants.

At the end of this period, after numerous unsuccessful attempts discussed in Goldin (1994), the federal government finally passed a literacy test for potential immigrants. The Immigration Act of 1917 required that any migrant over 16 years old had to be able to read between 30 and 40 words in a language of the potential immigrant's choosing. Figure 4.3 shows a card that would be used in this test, containing a bible verse, printed in Turkish with Armenian script (top) and in English, which would be presented to Armenian immigrants from Turkey at Ellis Island.

Note that what language the modal immigrant would have chosen to read changed dramatically between 1880 and 1910; in the 1880 Census immigrants from Southern, Central, and Eastern Europe made up fewer than 10% of all immigrants, but by the 1910 Census they were closer to 70%. The consequences for failing the literacy test were stark. Not only would an immigrant who failed the test be denied entry into the USA, but also the owners of the boat he came on would be fined $200 (roughly $4,000 in 2015), a large enough sum that transportation companies likely began administering the test prior to boarding (Goldin, 1994).

A literacy test, in some form or another, had been debated and actually passed in one or both houses of Congress more than ten times since 1897, when roughly 25% of all immigrants and 40% of 'newer' immigrants were unlikely to have passed (Goldin, 1993). Final passage of a literacy test is attributed in large part to a shift in voting patterns in southern states, potentially due to a desire to deprive northern cities of population (note that this occurred during a time when black Americans were beginning to leave the southern USA for northern cities) and/or concern that new groups of people immigrating were not obviously white enough (Goldin, 1994). The other primary political proponents of unrestricted immigration were US business owners. Even after the ACLL prohibited direct recruitment of foreigners, and consistent with most immigrants being relatively risk tolerant as a general rule, new arrivals from abroad provided a steady stream of relatively low-wage labour for US businesses during the second half of the nineteenth century. However, the rise of unions, communism, and occasionally violent labour strikes in the 1890s led industry leaders to finally support more stringent ex ante restrictions on who could enter the country (Higham, 1955).

In some ways, the literacy test was also a form of what is now called 'race neutral discrimination' (Spann, 2004); Massachusetts Senator Henry Cabot Lodge was, infamously, very clear about who would be affected by the test: 'the Italians, Russians, Poles, Hungarians, Greeks, and Asiatics.' Of course, these groups were explicitly targeted four years later with the Emergency Quota Act of 1921, but the text of the Act of 1917 does not mention nationality. In further evidence that the literacy test was more about restricting the entry of specific racial groups rather than literacy per se, exemptions from the literacy test were carved out for Mexicans, who were allowed temporary work permits under the precursor of the Bracero Program between 1917 and 1921, regardless of their ability to read. Exceptions were also made for the dependents of already admitted immigrants: a legally admitted immigrant was allowed to 'send for his father or grandfather over fifty-five years of age, his wife, his mother, his grandmother, or his unmarried or widowed daughter', who would be admitted regardless of their literacy.

In terms of its implications for the criminality of immigrants, the literacy test should have direct, albeit perhaps unintended, effects. The historical record suggests that literacy was, at the time, essentially a proxy for race and the 'right' kind of immigrant. In the most basic models of crime, race has at most an indirect role, typically as a proxy for some other more meaningful characteristic such as the probability of experiencing discrimination in the labour market (Pager, 2003). Literacy, on the other hand, directly affects human capital and the return to formal labour. Within the same gender, age category, and physical location, if 100% of immigrants and 70% of natives are literate, economic theory unambiguously predicts a higher crime rate among natives. We will return to a more detailed analysis of the Literacy Act of 1917 in the next section.

4.1.3 The Pet Door: 1920–50

The Literacy Act of 1917 ushered in the 'Pet Door' period of US immigration policy, during which legal immigration was essentially closed off to all but a few groups. As documented in Higham (1955), the Emergency Quota Act of 1921 was passed in response to a combination of economic crises, fear of foreign radicals, and also the continued flow of immigrants from non-Western Europe. The 1921 Act fixed annual lawful immigration from each country at 3% of the total number of residents in the USA in the 1910 Census. In 1924, the threshold was lowered to 2% of the population, and the relevant Census pushed further back in time to 1890. Moving the Census backwards arguably had a larger impact on immigration than lowering the percentage threshold; 1897 was the year at which 'new' immigrants from Eastern and Southern Europe outnumbered by those from Western Europe and Scandinavia (Meyers, 2004). The Immigration Act of 1924 can be thought of as an attempt to force the composition of immigrants thirty years backwards. Of course, this resulted in immigrant visas designated for favoured countries going unused, and thousands of people from less desirable countries,

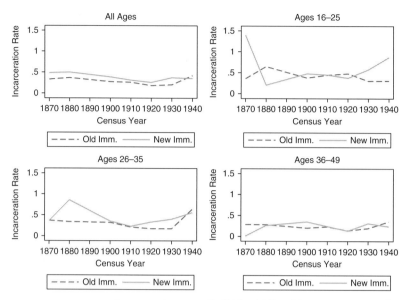

FIGURE 4.4 Incarceration rates (in %) for 'old' and 'new' immigrants, by age group, 1870–1940.

including children attempting to flee the Holocaust, being turned away.[3]

As Figure 4.4 shows, the justification that newer immigrants were somehow morally inferior to the older immigrants groups is not obviously supported by crime data available at the time. Prior to 1920, 'older' immigrants from Western Europe or Scandinavia were slightly over-represented in prisons relative to immigrants from 'newer' places among people of peak criminal age. New immigrants between 26 and 35 years of age were more criminal than older immigrants, suggesting that settlement patterns likely complicate direct comparisons, as they did in the case of Asian immigrants in the 1800s. Among the oldest groups 'new' immigrants are about as criminal as 'old' ones.

[3]   In 1938, New York senator Robert Wagner and Massachusetts representative Edith Rogers sponsored a bill that would relax these quotes and allow 20,000 Jewish German children under the age of 14 to enter the USA over a period of two years. North Carolina senator Robert Rice Reynolds blocked the bill from being considered, ostensibly because the admission of these children would be a distraction from the issue of domestic child poverty (Pleasants, 2000).

Notably, however, 1920 is a year of inflection. In 1920, 1930, and 1940, 'new' immigrants under 35 have the highest incarceration rates of any group. In terms of magnitude, the differences are relatively small – less than one-fifth of a percentage point. For men between 36 and 45, 'new' immigrants are best characterized as equally criminal to natives after 1900.

As with the 1917 Literacy Act, the only exceptions to the Immigration Act of 1924 were reserved for temporary agricultural workers from Mexico. The Mexican Agricultural Labour Program, known as the Bracero Program, was formally in effect from 1942 to 1964. A joint effort of the State Department, the Department of Labour, and the Immigration and Naturalization Service (INS), the Bracero program was basically a return to the Contract Labour Law of 1864; companies, typically in agriculture or railroad construction, were allowed to recruit a fixed number of Mexican workers. In exchange for this right, the hiring firms were required to provide workers with a basic level of wages, housing, and food, although there was limited enforcement of these requirements. Mexican people who finished their Bracero contract were supposed to return to Mexico. However, there is general agreement among historians that many stayed in the USA without permanent visas, and US farmers, Texans in particular, could use the Mexican contacts they made through Bracero to attract and employ Mexican workers outside of the program (Garcia, 1980; Martin, 2003).

The federal government's explicit ban on immigrants from Asian countries began to soften with the start of World War II. Once China became an official ally of the United States, the Magnuson Act of 1943 repealed the Chinese Exclusion Act of 1882. While the Magnuson Act did allow Chinese people living in the USA to become citizens, and allowed for the possibility of Chinese immigration, the quotas set up by the Immigration Act of 1924 were still in place, limiting the number of available visas to just over 100 a year. The War Brides Act of 1945 initially prohibited Filipino or Indian wives from entering the USA, but this restriction was removed in 1946.

4.1.4   The Dutch Door: 1950–2001

As the post–World War II political climate transitioned into the Cold War, immigration policies became one of many potential tools that could be used for propaganda and geopolitical leverage. A series of acts passed between 1948 and 1966 had the effect of eliminating the 1924 quotas for European people displaced by the war or fleeing communism. People from Vietnam, Cambodia, and Laos were also given special status in 1975 under the Indochina Migration and Refugee Assistance Act. Under the 1966 Cuban Adjustment Program, Cuban people living in the USA could become permanent residents after living in the USA for two years (reduced to one year in 1976).

For people from countries further from the edges of the communist Iron Curtain, changes in immigration policy had a different trend. In 1954, the INS and US Attorney General's office, in cooperation with the Mexican government, began the controversial Operation Wetback. Under this program, INS officers actively sought out 'criminal types from Mexico' (Ngai, 2004, p. 149) who were not living in the United States in compliance with the Bracero program. In 1954, about 1 million people were apprehended by US law enforcement officials (Garcia, 1980), and most were subsequently transported to southern and central Mexico. The deportations happened quickly, and as a result the program was arguably less well targeted than it could have been, in the sense that legal US residents of Mexican descent were caught up in the raids (Garcia, 1980), and the program itself was poorly administered; in one event, 88 Mexican people died of heatstroke after being deposited in the desert, and a congressional investigation referred to boats used to transport people to Mexico as 'penal hell ships' (Ngai, 2004, p. 156). Census data suggest that, while immigration from Mexico continued to increase between 1940 and 1970, the propensity of those immigrants to commit crimes plummeted as Operation Wetback rolled out. In fact, in the 1950 Census, young male migrants from Mexico were at least four times more likely to be behind bars than similarly aged natives living in the same places. In

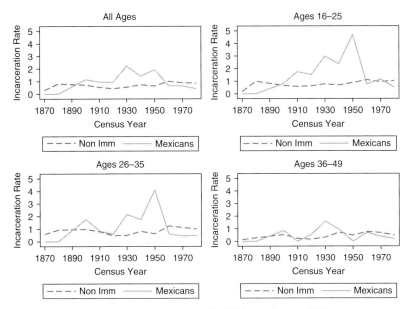

FIGURE 4.5 Incarceration rates (in %) for natives and Mexican immigrants, by age group, 1870–1980.

1960, incarceration rates plummeted to as low as one-half the rate of natives.

This dramatic reduction in incarceration rates is consistent with two mechanisms. First, Operation Wetback may have reduced the fraction of Mexican immigrants in prisons through selective incapacitation – removing people prone to criminal activity from the population. This was, of course, the stated goal of the program. Second, the high-profile raids could have had a strong deterrent impact on Mexicans living in the USA, with the very real threat of deportation increasing the cost of crime.

Of course, the broadest change in ex ante immigration policy occurred in 1965, when the Immigration Act of 1952 was amended to repeal the 1924 quotas. In place of the old quotas, priority for visas was given to immigrants who were related to US citizens, or who had secured employment in the USA. Shifting immigration priorities from promoting a specific racial and ethnic mix to one focused on promoting human capital (either through strengthening families or matching workers with firms) resulted in a dramatic change in the composition of immigrants. In the 1970 Census, more than 22% of the immigrant population was born in the Americas or Asia, compared with 12% in the 1960 Census and 7% in 1950. Further, since 1960, the incarceration rate of immigrants has been below that of their native-born neighbours.

This pattern of under-representation in prisons is well documented among first-generation immigrants, and Butcher and Piehl (2007) identify two US policies that are likely responsible for this difference: First, the 1965 Immigration Act, in some sense, defined 'desirable' immigrants as those who either were interested in working in the USA or wanted to reunite with family members. Rather than discouraging anyone from a particular set of countries to enter, official US policy identified individuals who wished to increase their human or social capital by immigrating, both of which are features associated with lower propensity to engage in crime. Second, the waiting period between entry and citizenship, during which immigrants had to demonstrate their sound moral character or be deported, increased the cost of punishment for immigrants relative to natives, meaning that the expected cost of crime was higher for new arrivals.

Empirically, the long-run impact that the 1965 Immigration Act had on the composition of immigrants is somewhat contested. Borjas (1995) argues that the human capital of immigrants has been declining over time relative to that of natives, pointing to a reduction in relative educational attainment after 1970. However, Census data on institutionalization do not suggest that the criminality of immigrants rose from 1970 to 2000. While changes in Census survey design make it difficult to track the incarceration rate of immigrants after 1980, the consistent rate at which immigrants live in group quarters may suggest that, even if immigrants as a group appear to have lower levels of human capital along measures we can observe (such as years of formal education), these may be offset by higher levels of human capital that are more difficult to measure (such as grit or empathy).

With the exception of refugee acts which, as previously discussed, targeted people living in communist countries as part of what Meyers (2004) identifies as geopolitical manoeuvring, the next major change in US immigration policy was enacted in 1986: the Immigration Reform and Control Act of 1986, or IRCA.

IRCA had three broad components. First, it increased spending on border control, by increasing the budget of the INS, and authorized additional hiring of officers along the northern and southern borders of the USA. Second, IRCA required that all US employers verify the immigration status of anyone they hired after 1 November 1986 and report this information to the INS. Failure to do so was considered a federal criminal offense. This was a substantial change from previous employer rules about hiring people who had entered the country without authorization to work, which before IRCA would have resulted in a civil citation, similar to a health code violation (Freedman et al., 2018). Third, IRCA granted amnesty to people who could document living and working in the USA, without violating any criminal laws, for a substantial period of time. Prior to IRCA's enactment, it was estimated that 1.3 to 2.7 million people would be eligible for temporary visitor status, and eventual citizenship, through the Legally Authorized Workers (LAW) amnesty programs, and the INS expected 800,000 Special Agricultural Worker (SAW) program applications (Hoefer et al., 1991). In fact, just over 3 million people applied, 1.76 through LAW, and 1.27 through SAW. By 2001, 2.7 million people gained permanent resident status, and 900,000 people were granted citizenship by IRCA (Rytina, 2002).

In addition to the sheer number of people affected, IRCA was also differentiated from previous immigration laws in that it represented a shift toward ex post restrictions on immigrant behaviour, through its regulation and surveillance of employers, rather than the immigrants themselves. Of course, previous federal immigration policies included ex post restrictions, such as waiting periods, and state laws restricting the ability of immigrants to own property also affected the incentives of immigrants in the country. However, IRCA's lasting legacy was not a wall at the border, or a new set of ex ante restrictions on the types of people allowed to enter the country, but the federal I-9 form that all people working in the USA must fill out when starting a new job. Prior to IRCA, undocumented workers seemed to suffer little wage penalty relative to documented immigrants, conditional on time in the USA and education (Massey, 1987). After 1986, workers without I-9 forms on file with their employer earned 24% less than those who did have a valid taxpayer identification number (Kossoudji and Cobb-Clark, 2002).

Since IRCA, a number of US policies have added to ex post immigration restrictions. People without documentation are not eligible for social insurance programs such as public housing, food assistance, or cash welfare programs, and non-citizens who are lawfully present in the USA have periodically had restricted access to these programs; between 1996 and 2002, non-citizens were ineligible for any federal assistance, and currently legal residents who are non-citizens must wait for one to five years before becoming eligible.[4]

The impact that these restrictions have had on the lives of immigrants increased in 2002, when the federal government began entering into '287(g)' partnerships with local law enforcement agencies. Named for the relevant subsection of the Immigrant and Nationality Act, amendment 287(g) allowed local law enforcement agencies to enforce federal immigration laws, meaning the officers could arrest someone they suspected of violating immigration laws rather than any state criminal law. This amendment to federal law was made in 1996, but only in 2002, after the terrorist attacks of 11 September 2001, did any partnerships actually occur, and in 2007 the number of agreements increased dramatically.

Placing restrictions on the ability of immigrants to work or receive social insurance has proved to be a politically popular way of controlling immigration; according to a 2011 survey, the plurality of Americans felt that such ex post restrictions on the behaviour of

---

[4]   There are some exceptions for 'emergency' situations, for the most part when children are affected.

immigrants was the best way to reduce the problems associated with illegal immigration (Transatlantic Trends, 2011). Policies that relax these ex post regulations, such as the 2001 Development, Relief, and Education for Alien Minors Act, which would provide a pathway to citizenship for people who entered the country illegally before they were 18, or state-level policies that allow undocumented residents to enroll in college at in-state prices, are highly controversial.

4.1.5   Does the Immigration Regime Matter?

In general, ex ante immigration restrictions had at least one of three policy goals: to restrict population growth during economic down-turns, to support US foreign policy goals, or to placate xenophobic fears after a shift in the (real or perceived) composition of immigrants. Ex ante restrictions could change the behaviour of immigrants on average by changing who the typical immigrant is – an Irishman, a Mexican, or a Swede? Ex post policy changes are distinct from ex ante restrictions in that not only will they tend to change the composition of who immigrates, but they will also influence how Irishmen, Mexicans, or Swedes behave once they are in the country. Policies limiting employment opportunities, prohibiting civic participation, withholding social support, or denying investment opportunities for new arrivals may also change the relative costs and benefits of participating in illegal activity for the affected immigrants.

The relationship between immigration and crime in the USA will therefore be related to both the ex ante and ex post policies in place. Restrictive ex ante policies, such as literacy tests or head taxes, will tend to make immigrants less criminal through compositional change; by preventing people who have low levels of human capital and/or low incomes from entering the country, ex ante policies can 'screen out' individuals who have characteristics that are positively correlated with crime. Implementing ex post immigration control, on the other hand, may serve to increase or decrease criminality of immigrants without necessarily changing who the immigrants are. Longer waiting periods for citizenship increase the expected cost of committing a crime or engaging in deviant behaviour. In a series of papers using historical Census data on state prisoners between 1900 and 1930, a time period when the predominant federal immigration policies were either ex ante screens or ex post waiting periods, Moehling and Piehl (2009), and Moehling and Piehl (2014) document that, among men over 20, immigrants were either equally likely, or much less likely, to be incarcerated than natives at any age group, and immigrants in general became less likely to be incarcerated over the sample period. Contemporaneous accounts of high rates of incarceration among immigrant groups can be attributed to, essentially, a failure to adequately and flexibly control for the different age distributions of the immigrant and native populations (Moehling and Piehl, 2014).[5]

Since 1986, US immigration policy has placed more emphasis on ex post restrictions that limit opportunities for new arrivals, rather than simply limiting arrivals. As a result of this change, one would expect the relationship between immigration and crime to also change over time. Modern research on ex post immigration restrictions in the USA, along with restrictions in Italy, and the UK discussed earlier in this book, in the late part of the twentieth and early twenty-first centuries, has found evidence that limiting (or expanding) employment opportunities for immigrants has increased (or decreased) their participation in criminal activity (e.g. Bell and Machin, 2013; Mastrobuoni and Pinotti, 2015; Freedman et al., 2018; Pinotti, 2017).

We provide complementary evidence to this research by documenting incarceration rates, by age, based on decennial Census data from 1870 to 1950. As America adjusted its ex post and ex ante immigration policies, we will look for similar shifts in the relative incarceration rates of natives and the foreign born. Figure 4.6 displays the weighted incarceration rates for natives and non-native men, in

---

[5] At the same time, however, immigrants during this time period were not a homogeneous group. Bodenhorn et al. (2010) found evidence that immigrants living in urban areas were generally less likely than local natives to be incarcerated, although in rural areas, immigrants were incarcerated at higher rates than natives.

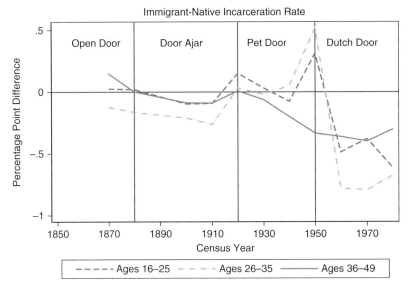

FIGURE 4.6 Incarceration rates (in %) for native and non-native men, by age (1870–1980), along with major immigration reforms.

every Census from 1870 to 1980, by age, along with major immigration reforms.

It is clear that, in almost every year, immigrants as a whole are less likely to be in prison than natives. Only during the end of the 'Pet Door' era, when ex ante policies placed strict limits on the legal immigration of people from certain countries, do we observe a consistent over-representation of young men in correctional facilities. After the 'Dutch Door' period began, when the ex post Operation Wetback actively sought out 'criminal' Mexican immigrants, and ex ante policies became based on human and social capital, rather than nationality, immigrant incarceration rates fall to their lowest levels in US history.

4.2 THE 1917 IMMIGRATION ACT

The 1917 Immigration Act required that all adult males who migrated to the USA pass a literacy test. As mentioned previously, all men over the age of 16 had to read a passage of 30 to 40 words, in the language of their choosing, to demonstrate that they were capable of reading. Similar to previous acts, the act also categorically excluded 'idiots, imbeciles, and feeble-minded persons'; persons of 'constitutional psychopathic inferiority'; 'mentally or physically defective' persons, as well as the insane, alcoholics, and criminals. The period of time during which immigrants could be deported was lengthened from three years to five years, and the deportable classes now included aliens convicted of crimes and sentenced to imprisonment of one year or more. On docking in the USA, ships carrying immigrants were required to provide Immigration officials detailed information about each passenger's name, age, sex, physical description, literacy, nationality, destination, occupation, mental and physical health, as well as information about their criminal record.

The clear purpose of the 1917 Act was to try to create a better pool of immigrants – more literate, more productive, and less criminogenic. The IPUMS samples of the 1910, 1920, and 1930 US Censuses allow us to assess whether the act did indeed change the composition of migrants. These Censuses contain information about the year that an immigrant entered the USA, allowing for a fairly detailed analysis of the evolution of illiteracy and incarceration rates depending on whether immigrants migrated before or after 1917.

The act was passed on 1 February and became fully effective by that May. However, there is evidence that it took additional months for the necessary infrastructure to be put in place. Immigrants had to be literate in *any* language, which meant that the reading test had to be prepared in all languages, and that immigration officers had to be prepared enough to understand whether the reading was actually correct.

The 1910, 1920, and 1930 Censuses asked respondents about their ability to read and write. Table 4.2 shows that in 1910, about 6% of the natives between the ages of 16 and 49 were illiterate, compared to 21% of people born outside the USA. By 1930 the numbers dropped to 3% and 9%, respectively, implying that the 1917 Act may have reduced immigrant illiteracy rates by more than 50%.

Table 4.2 *Incarceration rates for foreign and native-born by Census year and illiteracy status*

		1910		1920		1930	
		Literate	Illiterate	Literate	Illiterate	Literate	Illiterate
Native born	incarceration rate	0.39%	1.00%	0.32%	1.34%	0.71%	1.92%
	pop. (in m.)	18.20	1.22	21.30	1.02	52.60	1.75
	fraction	0.94	0.06	0.95	0.05	0.97	0.03
Foreign born	incarceration rate	0.27%	0.45%	0.26%	0.40%	0.34%	0.45%
	pop. (in m.)	2.06	0.54	2.59	0.52	5.86	0.60
	fraction	0.79	0.21	0.83	0.17	0.91	0.09

As previously discussed, literacy is typically thought to be directly related to crime, as it is an observable measure of human capital. Census data from this time period suggest that the strength of this connection may vary for immigrants and natives. Among literate individuals in 1910, incarceration rates were almost identical between native and foreign born. We do not observe the same relationship for illiterate individuals; illiterate natives were twice as likely to be incarcerated as illiterate immigrants. In other words, even though illiterate immigrants may be able to earn low market wages, there is something unobservable about them that lowers their propensity to commit crime compared to natives.

These differences in the relationship between literacy and criminality became even more extreme over time. In 1920, the incarceration rate among illiterate aliens was almost the same as those who were literate, which was almost one-fourth the incarceration rate of illiterate natives. By 1930, illiterate immigrants were almost one-fifth as likely to be incarcerated (0.45% vs. 1.92%) as an illiterate native, and even literate immigrants were less likely to be incarcerated compared to literate natives (0.34% vs. 0.71%). One explanation for this declining criminality among low-skilled immigrants is the well-

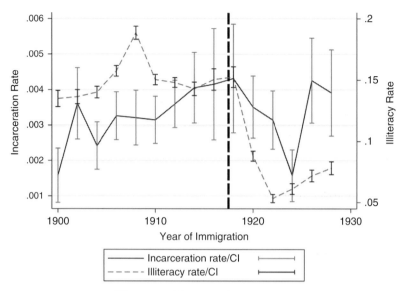

FIGURE 4.7 Illiteracy and incarceration rates.

established link between criminality and age. To the extent that the literacy requirement was enforced, immigrants who could not read should have immigrated prior to 1917, while literate immigrants could have entered the country at any time. As a result, in the 1920 and 1930 Censuses, literacy may be a proxy for date of immigration. Since date of immigration is also correlated with age, this would mean that, after 1917, illiterate immigrants are likely to be older than literate ones, on average, and thus also less criminal.

When focusing on foreign-born individuals, one can follow the evolution of their literacy and incarceration rates across years of immigration. Using information from three different Censuses, Figure 4.7 shows that, prior to 1918, both illiteracy and incarceration rates of immigrants are slowly trending upwards.[6] Then, in 1918, illiteracy rates drop from about 15% to about 5%, and incarceration

---

6   Averages are computed every two years to reduce the sampling variation driven by the low incarceration rates.

rates drop from about 4 per 1,000 to about 1.5 per 1,000. A few years later, both series start drifting upwards.[7]

Consistent with the racially based motivations previously discussed, the 1917 Act should have differentially affected migrants from different countries. We confirm that this did, in fact, occur, with two important exceptions, Italy and Mexico. Table 4.3 shows that immigrant populations with the largest pre-1917 illiteracy rates, with the exception of Italy and Mexico, swathe the largest drops in population. There is also a clear reduction in incarceration numbers, possibly due to the improved literacy.

Figure 4.8 plots the changes in the fraction of migrants coming from each country (with circles proportional to the pre-1917 fraction), against the initial rates of illiteracy.[8] Overall, a regression line that is weighted by the size of immigrant population of each country is fairly flat (dashed line), but this is driven by two countries that were not subject to strict enforcement, namely Mexico and Italy. Excluding the two countries the line becomes negatively sloped (dotted line). As previously discussed, Mexican agricultural workers were exempt from the literacy requirements. The lack of enforcement among Italian immigrants might be driven by the fact that, between 1900 and 1917, most immigrants were Italian, and immediate dependent family members of immigrants who were already living in the USA were also exempt. Another factor might have contributed to a more lax enforcement is the multitude of Italian dialects and languages that

---

[7] There is considerably more noise (the vertical line shows the 95% confidence intervals) in incarceration rates compare to illiteracy rates. This is probably driven by three factors. First, both rates are measured at the time of the surveys and illiteracy is likely to be a more persistent trait compared to incarceration. Second, incarceration rates are close to zero, which increases its noise, as a few more or less incarcerated individuals can alter the rate considerably. Finally, it would probably take time for the literacy effects to show up in incarceration rates. Criminals would have had to be arrested, convicted, and finally incarcerated, which would take time. The last point is a plausible explanation for why incarceration rates appear to follow illiteracy rates with a slight lag.

[8] The change in the fraction for country c is computed as $\dfrac{\frac{\text{imm}_{c,\text{post}}}{\sum_c \text{imm}_{c,\text{post}}} - \frac{\text{imm}_{c,\text{pre}}}{\sum_c \text{imm}_{c,\text{pre}}}}{\frac{1}{2}\sum_c \text{imm}_{c,\text{post}} + \frac{1}{2}\sum_c \text{imm}_{c,\text{pre}}}$. Dividing by the average fraction of population avoids dividing by very small numbers.

Table 4.3 *Incarceration rates and illiteracy rates by country of birth*

Immigrants country of origin	Population (%)		Illiterate (%)		Incarceration (%)	
	Pre-1917	Post-1917	Pre-1917	Post-1917	Pre-1917	Post-1917
North America (excl. USA)	3.2	9.6	4.0	2.2	0.64	0.18
Central/South America	5.6	17.2	28.0	28.1	1.12	0.48
Asia	4.2	6.1	16.2	14.5	0.36	0.29
Italy	16.5	19.9	21.8	15.6	0.34	0.19
Poland	15.7	4.0	18.5	7.5	0.22	0.60
England	3.0	5.7	0.2	0.7	0.16	0.00
Ireland	3.2	3.3	1.1	0.2	0.27	0.10
Greece	4.6	2.9	10.9	7.0	0.44	0.00
Germany	3.7	1.7	1.5	2.7	0.18	0.00
Rest of Europe	40.0	29.1	13.0	6.5	0.38	0.29
Other in the world	0.1	0.4	12.7	0.8	0.00	0.00

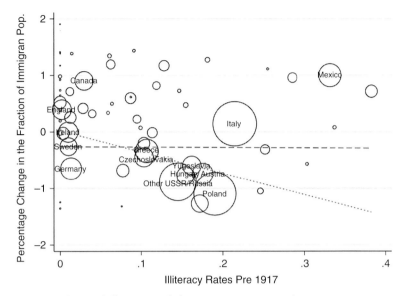

FIGURE 4.8 Initial illiteracy and changes in migrant population.

were spoken at the time, which might have complicated the administration of the literacy test.

We disentangle the impact of the change in the literacy of the immigrant population and the change in the composition of where the immigrants came from in a regression framework. This allows us to compare incarceration and literacy rates over time, controlling for other socio-economic characteristics. In particular, we estimate the following linear probability model:

$$\text{OUTCOME}_i = \delta_{\text{age}} + \delta_{\text{country of birth}} + \delta_{\text{state}} + \delta_{\text{year of birth}}$$

$$+ \theta\,\text{POST\_1917}_i + \beta'X_i + \epsilon_i,$$

We are interested in two binary outcomes: whether or not the Census respondent is illiterate, and whether or not the respondent is incarcerated. We want to differentiate the impact of the 1917 Act from the respondent's state of residence, age, Census year, country of birth, year of immigration, gender, race, and Hispanic origin, so we include controls for all of these variables in the matrix X_i.

In this framework, θ measures the changes in literacy or incarceration after 1917, taking into account differences in these factors across individuals. In other words, we test whether individuals who appear to be similar to each other with respect to several characteristics but differ by whether they migrated before or after 1917 have different illiteracy and incarceration rates. The results are shown in Table 4.4.

In panel A, the outcome variable is illiteracy, and we find that illiteracy among immigrants fell by 7.8 percentage points after the 1917 Act was passed. Because the test itself was phased in over the course of 1917, and perhaps 1918, in the next columns we exclude those years, and find a slightly bigger effect – just over a 9 percentage point reduction in illiteracy. Including our additional controls for gender and race yields roughly similar results, as does excluding people who entered the country in the year they were surveyed. In other words, Census data suggest that the 1917 Act did increase the probability that an immigrant could read.

In panel B we examine how incarceration rates changed after immigrants were subject to the 1917 Act. While the coefficient on the post-1917 dummy is always negative, suggesting that people who immigrated after 1917 were less likely to be convicted of crimes, it is not statistically significant unless we exclude people who entered the country in 1917 or 1918. Excluding these years yields larger estimates of the impact of the law on illiteracy, but also may reflect measurement error in our estimate of criminality. For someone to be labelled a criminal in the Census data, the person would not only have had to have committed a crime, but also to have been arrested, convicted, and incarcerated, a process that takes time.

Excluding the first two years after the 1917 Act was passed generates a fairly strong negative relationship between the policy and incarceration. Controlling for just year of birth and age suggests that the 1917 Act lowered incarceration rates by 1.5 percentage points,

Table 4.4 *Illiterate and incarceration regressions*

	(1)	(2)	(3)	(4)	(5)
Migration years	All	No 1917	All	No 1917 and 1918	All
Years since migration	All	All	All	All	>0
Panel A: First stage, dep. var. illiterate					
Post-1917	-0.0782***	-0.0859***	-0.0961***	-0.0681***	-0.0654***
	(0.0167)	(0.0169)	(0.0167)	(0.0103)	(0.0093)
Year of immigration	0.0070***	0.0073***	0.0076***	0.0073***	0.0070***
	(0.0020)	(0.0020)	(0.0020)	(0.0015)	(0.0013)
R^2	0.0288	0.0292	0.0298	0.1037	0.1011
Mean dep. Var	0.114	0.114	0.114	0.114	0.112
Panel B: Reduced form, dep. var. incarceration					
Post-1917	-0.0010	-0.0011	-0.0015**	-0.0017**	-0.0018**
	(0.0007)	(0.0007)	(0.0006)	(0.0008)	(0.0008)
Year of immigration	-0.0000	-0.0000	0.0000	-0.0000	-0.0000
	(0.0001)	(0.0001)	(0.0000)	(0.0001)	(0.0000)
R^2	0.0008	0.0008	0.0008	0.0032	0.0033
Mean dep. Var	0.00340	0.00337	0.00332	0.00332	0.00334
Year of birth FE	Yes	Yes	Yes	Yes	Yes
Age in Census yr. FE	Yes	Yes	Yes	Yes	Yes
Other Xs				Yes	Yes
Observations	248,566	245,975	243,366	243,365	241,728

Note: Panels A and B show results of standard OLS regressions. In panel A, the dependent variable is illiteracy, while in panel B, the dependent variable is the incarceration rate. Standard errors in parentheses.

$^* p < 0.1$; $^{**} p < 0.05$; $^{***} p < 0.01$.

or about 50%. Adding the other controls further strengthens the relationship, as does excluding immigrants who arrived in the USA the year of the survey (thus hardly having the time to end up in prison). By placing ex ante restrictions on the human capital of immigrants, the 1917 Act likely played an important role in raising the 'moral character' of immigrants.

4.3   THE 1986 IMMIGRATION REFORM AND CONTROL ACT

The 1965 revocation of the 1924 National Origins Act ushered in the 'Dutch Door' period of immigration policy, and dramatically changed the path of US immigration. After four decades of relatively slow decline, the 1980 Census revealed that the number of immigrants living in the USA increased by 40%, from just under 10 million in 1970 to over 14 million. This was almost the same number of foreign-born people living in the USA in the 1930 Census, before the total impact of the 1920s quotas began to chip away at the number of migrants.

Not only did the rate of immigration continue to increase after 1970, but also the composition of these new immigrants was dramatically different than in past years, with people from Mexico, Central America, and Asia increasingly entering the country. Some fraction of these new arrivals entered the country after properly registering with the INS and receiving legal authorization to live and work in the USA, but others crossed land or sea borders surreptitiously, or legally entered as tourists or students and simply stayed on. Without visas allowing them to work, these immigrants were unable to provide the taxpayer identification or Social Security numbers employers needed to remit payroll taxes to state and federal governments. Instead, undocumented workers held jobs where they were paid under-the-table by employers willing to risk the associated fines if they were discovered.

After several years of public debate about these new waves of immigrants, particularly those without legal authorization to work, Congress passed the Immigration Reform and Control Act of 1986 (IRCA 1986). There were essentially two components of

IRCA. First, IRCA attempted to stem the flow of undocumented immigrants into the USA through ex ante and ex post measures: the budget of the INS was increased to help them enforce border controls, and the expected penalties for employers who hired undocumented workers were significantly increased; as of 1 November 1986, employers who knowingly hired such workers were subject to criminal sanctions, and employers were required to proactively file paperwork documenting the legal status of all employees hired after that date. The second component of IRCA addressed one of the oldest concerns about the immigrants currently in the country: that they would not become 'American' and fully integrate themselves into society. To promote this, IRCA also introduced two programs through which long time, non-criminal, undocumented residents could become citizens.

Beginning in May of 1987, anyone who could attest that they had been continuously living in the United States since 1 January 1982 could register with an INS field office and obtain temporary legal resident status through the Legally Authorized Workers (LAW) program. This temporary status allowed them to legally work and also, eventually, to become a US citizen. Alternately, someone who had regularly worked in agriculture for at least ninety days could apply for the same status through the Special Agricultural Workers (SAW) program. Applications for these programs, which could be submitted in person or through third parties such as church groups, were accepted through May of 1988 (LAW) and November of 1988 (SAW).

While more than thirty years old, the legacy of IRCA still dominates policy discussions as one of the largest 'shocks' to immigration policy in US history. More than 2.7 million immigrants, largely from Mexico, obtained legal status through this program, although many likely did not technically meet either LAW or SAWs requirements; one highly cited study estimates that more than 70% of LAW applications and 40% of SAW applications were fraudulent (Donato and Carter, 1999).

As previously discussed, immigrants who did not obtain legal status through LAW or SAW did face more difficulty in the job market after IRCA (Bansak and Raphael, 2001; Donato et al., 1992a; Donato and Massey, 1993; Rivera-Batiz, 1999; Kossoudji and Cobb-Clark, 2002). However, the extent to which this deterred people from entering the country is unclear. Both small-scale surveys of border crossing points and large-scale surveys conducted in Mexico and the USA find that the ex ante and ex post IRCA restrictions on immigrants had minimal impact on the flow of immigrants into the USA (Bustamente, 1990; Woodrow and Passel, 1990; Donato et al., 1992b). INS apprehension data suggest that there may have been a short-term reduction in illegal immigration in the first few months of 1987, but immigrant flows quickly returned to their normal levels (Orrenius and Zavodny, 2003).

A few recent papers examine the impact that IRCA had on crime rates, a task which is complicated by available data. Decennial Census stopped differentiating correctional institutions from mental institutions, nursing homes, or assisted living facilities after the 1980 Census, and because immigration law is federal, rather than state policy, municipal police, county jails, and state prisons have little incentive to track the citizenship status of people they encounter. Further, while the plurality of people legalized through IRCA were Mexican, the FBI's authorization to collect information on the ethnicity of people who were arrested ended in 1986.

Research on the criminal activity of immigrants whose legal status changes with EU expansion has found that gaining authorization to work is associated with reductions in criminal activity (Mastrobuoni and Pinotti, 2015; Pinotti, 2017). Baker (2015) presents evidence consistent with this in the USA; areas where more immigrants gained citizenship status through IRCA, which tended to occur in the late 1980s and early 1990s, saw larger reductions in officially recorded crime. Freedman et al. (2018) focus on the expiration of the amnesty provisions of IRCA, and find that Hispanic

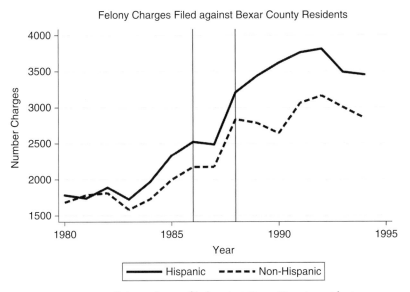

FIGURE 4.9 Felony charges filed against Bexar County residents.

people living in immigrant neighbourhoods in Texas were more likely to be accused of felonies after 1988. Figure 4.9 documents this jump. They attribute this to the reduction in job opportunities for remaining undocumented workers after the SAW and LAW programs ended.

Finally, Comino et al. (2016) highlights another important implication of immigration policy for crime rates. By formalizing and solidifying the relationship between the undocumented immigrant and the broader community, IRCA may have encouraged crime victims to notify the police. Using a similar strategy as Baker (2015), but using the National Crime Victimization Survey rather than aggregated Uniform Crime Reports, Comino et al. (2016) find that Hispanic crime victims were more likely to contact the police when they lived in cities where large fractions of the population gained citizenship, and were less likely to become crime victims. While the victimization survey does not contain information on immigrant status, the authors leverage the fact that individuals of Hispanic origin were two orders of

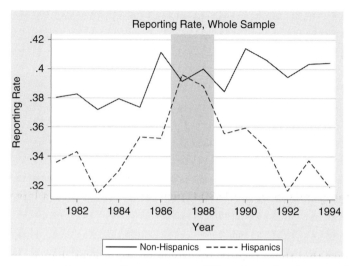

FIGURE 4.10 Reporting rates of Hispanics and natives around the IRCA.

magnitude more likely to apply for the amnesty when compared to those of non-Hispanic ones.

Figure 4.10 shows that victims of crimes who are non-Hispanic have fairly flat reporting rates around the years of the IRCA amnesty. This is not true for victims of crime who are of Hispanic origin. For them reporting rates peak in the years of the amnesty, when the fraction of undocumented immigrants is presumably at its lowest level, as later years had a continued influx of undocumented migrants from Mexico and other Central American countries.

4.4 CONCLUSIONS

We have documented how more than 250 years of US immigration policy may have influenced the link between immigration and crime. Immigration policy has gone through many different phases, from an almost liberalized 'Open Door' era from 1776 to 1880 when the federal immigration policies encouraged new arrivals; a 'Door Ajar' era from 1880 to 1920, where increasing nationality and human capital-based restrictions prevented certain groups of people from entering; to a highly restrictive 'Pet Door' era from 1920 to 1950 and a 'Dutch Door' era from 1950 to the present, which relaxed national quotas in favour of policies encouraging family reunification and high-skilled immigration.

The first anti-immigration policy that was driven by concerns about crime, the Chinese Exclusion Act of 1882, prohibited immigration from China until 1892, and issued deportation orders for all Chinese people who had entered the country after 17 November 1880. We do find evidence of Asian men being over-represented in prison in the 1880 Census and we also find a large drop in incarceration rates between 1880 and 1890. Yet, accounting for the fact that Chinese immigrants were mainly based in western states shows that these results are driven by state-level changes in incarceration rates rather than a different crime propensity between Asian and native men.

These ex ante policies aimed at selecting incoming migrants explicitly mentioned crime in the Immigration Act of 1882, which banned people with criminal histories from entering the USA. Incarceration rates for natives and non-natives are consistent with the hypothesis that the ex-ante prohibitions on criminals lead to a reduction in immigrant crime. The final ex ante policy of the 'Door Ajar' period introduced a stringent literacy test for incoming migrants. We show that resulting improvement in human capital led to important reductions in crime.

The Immigration Act of 1924, during the 'Pet Door' period, was another attempt to ex ante force the composition of immigrants thirty years backwards, giving priority to immigrants from Western Europe. There is no evidence that the resulting compositional change had any effect on immigrant crime.

A series of acts passed between 1948 and 1966, the early 'Dutch Door' period, had the effect of eliminating the 1924 quotas for European people displaced by the war or fleeing communism. But the one policy that in those years was driven by concerns about crime was 'Operation Wetback', an ex post immigration reform that the federal government started in 1954 in cooperation with the Mexican Government. INS officers would deport 'criminal types from Mexico' who were not in compliance with immigration law. That year about 1 million people were apprehended by US law enforcement officials and sent to Mexico. Census data suggest that between the 1950s and 1960s the propensity of those immigrants to commit crimes plummeted as Operation Wetback rolled out, especially among young immigrants.

The movement towards ex post immigration policies continued in 1965, when the Immigration Act of 1952 was amended to repeal the 1924 quotas and in 1986, when a massive immigration amnesty was passed. Empirical evidence from victimization surveys shows that, on one hand, immigrants who gained legal status became more likely to report crime to the police, and that made them less likely to be victims of crime. On the other hand, possibly because of the increased reporting and the reduction in job opportunities for the remaining undocumented workers after the SAW and LAW programs ended, there appears to have been an increase in crime by undocumented immigrants over the late 1980s and early 1990s.

The results of Comino et al. (2016) and Freedman et al. (2018) highlight the multilayered relationship between immigration policy and the criminal environment. While intended to prevent 'undesirable' criminal immigrants from entering, ex post policies that reduced the return to immigration may have the perverse effect of exacerbating the propensity of affected immigrants to engage in crime. At the same time, while there is scant evidence of public discussion of the need for undocumented immigrants to be protected from crime, when immigration policy embraces immigrants, as the conferral of citizenship status did, there is real evidence that crime victims are more likely to come forward and cooperate with police, reducing the 'dark shadow' of crime and making society safer as a whole.

5   Refugee Waves and Crime: Evidence from EU Countries

The European Union has experienced a major refugee crisis in the last few years. The total number of individuals with recognized refugee status who reside in one of the EU15 countries increased from approximately 1 million in 2014 to 1.8 million in 2016. Over the same period, the number of asylum applications received by EU15 countries increased from 500,000 in 2014 to more than 1 million in 2015 and to 1.1 million in 2016, reaching an unprecedented 2.6 million applications submitted in just three years. A large fraction of these applications are still being assessed to determine the status of the applicants.

The exposure to the flows of immigrants seeking humanitarian protection was extremely heterogeneous across EU countries. Figure 5.1 shows the number of asylum applications submitted in 2014, 2015, and 2016 and the refugee population in 2016 in each of the EU15 countries. Countries are ranked – in decreasing order – by their refugee population in 2016. Germany clearly bore the brunt of the crisis, receiving more than 1.3 million asylum claims in the between 2014 and 2016 and hosting about 670,000 refugees in 2016. France, Sweden, and Italy follow in the ranking, with a refugee population in 2016 of 300,000, 230,000, and 150,000 individuals, respectively. The same three countries come immediately after Germany – although in a slightly different order – when ranking the number of asylum applications received between 2014 and 2016: Italy (270,000), Sweden (250,000), and France (210,000). At the very end of the ranking we find Spain, Ireland, Luxembourg, and Portugal that host a few thousand refugees each and have collected a

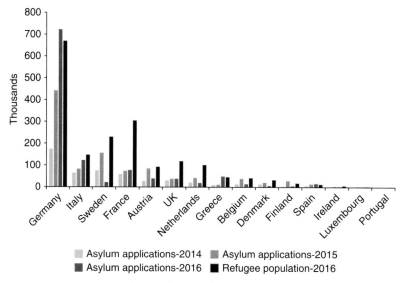

FIGURE 5.1 Asylum applications (2014–16) and refugee population (2016) in EU15 countries.

Note: The figure reports the number of asylum applications submitted in 2014, 2015, and 2016 and the refugee population in 2016 in EU15 countries. Countries are ranked by their refugee population in 2016 (in decreasing order).

Source: Authors' calculations from UNHCR records.

similarly small number of asylum claims in recent years. The extent to which different EU countries were affected by the 'refugee crisis' depends on a combination of geographical proximity to major entry routes and differences in implemented policies. The record high number of asylum applications in Germany, for instance, is largely explained by the decision of German chancellor Angela Merkel to suspend the Dublin Protocol for Syrian refugees in August 2015.[1] The suspension lasted approximately three months

---

[1]   The 1990 Dublin convention established the principle that the asylum seekers entering the EU can exclusively apply for asylum in the first member country they pass through. In 2000, the EU established a common asylum fingerprint database to enforce this principle. According to the convention, EU countries can refuse to consider the application of asylum seekers who have previously transited through other EU countries and forcedly remove them back to those countries.

and allowed Syrian citizens who were stranded in other EU countries to move to Germany and apply for asylum there.

The refugee crisis in Europe sparked an intense political debate on possible policy approaches to manage and reduce inflows and how to sustainably distribute asylum claimants across receiving countries (Fernández-Huertas Moraga and Rapoport, 2015; Hatton, 2015). As refugees continued to EU countries, the media and policy attention also gradually focused on the challenges posed by the socio-economic integration of refugees in hosting societies (Dustmann et al., 2017; Fasani et al., 2017).[2]

Refugees' potential involvement in crime was one of the concerns often mentioned in political debates, newspapers, and social media. Attitude survey data collected in spring 2016 in selected EU countries by the PEW Research Center identify three major concerns regarding refugees among citizens of hosting countries: crime, terrorism, and economic costs. The shares of respondents who report being concerned about refugees engaging in crime, increasing terrorism, and being an economic burden for hosting societies are illustrated in Figure 5.2. Concern about crime is widespread across European countries, being particularly high in Italy, Sweden, and Hungary, countries where more than 40% of the respondents voice that concern. In all countries, however, a substantially larger share of interviewees were worried about terrorism: in all countries surveyed but France and Spain, more than 50% of the respondents reported concerns about refugees increasing the likelihood of terrorist attacks in hosting societies. Similarly pervasive are the fears about the economic cost of refugees in terms of welfare benefits and increased labour market competition.

We know very little on whether asylum seekers and refugees display a higher propensity to engage in crime than comparable economic migrants or natives and on whether they may therefore lead to higher crime rates in receiving societies. From a theoretical

---

[2]   See Becker and Ferrara (forthcoming) for a recent and detailed review of evidence on refugees' impact on hosting societies.

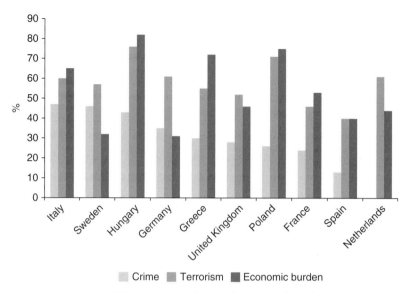

FIGURE 5.2 Major concerns about refugees in selected EU countries, 2016.

Note: The figure reports the shares of respondents in selected EU countries who reported being concerned about refugees engaging in crime, increasing terrorism, and being an economic burden for hosting societies. Countries are ranked based on the share of respondents concerned about crime involvement. The information on crime concern is not available for the Netherlands.

Source: Authors' calculations from PEW Research Center – Spring 2016 Global Attitudes Survey.

point of view, predictions are ambiguous and depend on the specific asylum policy framework they are subject to. The empirical evidence on the matter is also extremely scarce. In this chapter, we investigate whether EU countries that received larger inflows of people seeking humanitarian protection experienced statistically significant increases in their crime rates. To do so, we combine longitudinal national crime data and UN High Commissioner for Refugees (UNHCR) records on asylum seekers and refugee populations across EU countries from 1995 to 2016, and we carry out an original econometric analysis of the impact of refugees on crime rates.

The chapter has the following structure. In Section 5.2, we discuss theoretical predictions on refugees' propensity to engage in crime and review the existing empirical evidence. We then present the data used for our empirical analysis together with some descriptive statistics in Section 5.3. Section 5.4 provides a graphical analysis of the relation between the presence of asylum seekers and refugees and crime rates across EU countries. We discuss our empirical strategy in Section 5.5 and the findings are reported in Section 5.6. Section 5.7 concludes the chapter.

5.2 REFUGEES AND CRIME: THEORY AND EVIDENCE

Theory. The Becker (1968) model of criminal choice can be used to derive theoretical predictions regarding the criminal behaviour of asylum seekers and refugees. The discussion is similar to the one we developed on the role played by legal residence status in affecting immigrants' choices in the legal and illegal labour market (see the Introduction). Our reasoning should revolve around the effect of being an asylum seeker – and of being recognized as a refugee – on labour market opportunities, criminal opportunities, and potential penalties for engaging in crime.

It is reasonable to expect that asylum seekers will have a strong interest in avoiding any behaviour that may jeopardize their chances of being granted refugee status in the host country. They should therefore have low incentives to engage in crime. In most countries, however, while their applications are being processed, asylum seekers are typically unemployed and the benefits they receive from the government may be particularly low, which would tend to increase their incentives to engage in crime. Additional factors can further contribute to making their overall situation rather dire and challenging. The forced nature of refugee migration generally implies that individuals had little time to plan their migration and limited choice in selecting their destinations (see Borjas [2001] and Cadena and Kovak [2016] for evidence on the role of local labour market conditions in determining immigrant destinations). As a consequence, asylum seekers often arrive in countries where they have no good network of co-nationals and whose language they do not speak, complicating and delaying their socio-economic integration (Fasani et al., 2017). Moreover, asylum seekers were often exposed to violence and traumatic experiences, leading to relatively low levels of mental health (Porter and Haslam, 2005) that may eventually translate into antisocial behaviour. The combined effect of all these elements – poverty, marginalization, and distress – is potentially conducive to crime. Asylum policies can then play a major role in altering asylums seekers' incentives to commit crime. Waiting times for processing the application, refugee status recognition rates, restrictions on the labour market access of asylum seekers and refugees, and dispersal policies can all influence both the short- and the medium- to long-run socio-economic integration of refugees (Hainmueller et al., 2016; Fasani et al., 2017; Marbach et al., 2018), with potentially important consequences also for their criminal behaviour.

We can expect the effect of granting refugee status to asylum applicants to be somewhat analogous to the effect of granting legal status to undocumented immigrants. Being recognized as a refugee generally involves being offered permanent residence status in the host country, getting unrestricted access to its labour market and its welfare state, and experiencing a substantial reduction in overall uncertainty. Asylum seekers whose claim is rejected, instead, are potentially subject to detention and forced removal. If not forcibly removed, they generally join the undocumented population unless they find another way of getting legal residence status or move somewhere else. Insofar as obtaining refugee status leads to better labour market opportunities, we would expect it to be associated to lower propensity to engage in criminal behaviour. Other institutional features of the refugee status recognition process, however, make the net impact on criminal behaviour theoretically ambiguous. For example, newly recognized refugees generally lose their eligibility to any asylum support, which can include both cash and in-kind benefits.[3] Further, if the transition from asylum to regular benefits is not immediate and the individual is not employed, there may be a temporary income drop, which would increase incentives to commit crime. Finally, once permanent resident status in the host country is granted, refugees may commit more crime because of reduced deterrence (if they had feared that the approval of their application was contingent on their good behaviour).

Empirical evidence. A growing literature has studied the socio-economic integration of refugees in receiving countries, documenting the existence of a sizeable 'refugee gap' along a number of important socio-economic dimensions (see Bevelander [2016] for a review). Refugees tend to have significantly worse labour market outcomes than natives. Of course, being at a disadvantage vis-à-vis native workers is a common trait for immigrants in most hosting societies.[4] Refugees, however, tend to experience even weaker labour market outcomes than immigrants with very similar characteristics. A recent and comprehensive analysis of refugees' integration across EU15 countries is provided in Fasani et al. (2017). They analyse data from two waves of the European Union Labour Force Survey and show that refugees are 13% less likely to be employed than migrants with similar characteristics. When looking only at those who participate in the labour market, they find that refugees are 32% more likely to be unemployed than comparable migrants. They also document the presence of a negative refugee gap in other labour market outcomes (participation, occupational quality, income), in health, and in proficiency in the host country language. When looking at assimilation profiles, Fasani et al. (2017) found that the refugee gaps persist for about ten years after arrival in the host country. The persistence of the gaps is a common finding in the literature,

---

[3] In the UK, for instance, asylum support for asylum seekers who are given refugee status ends 28 days after the decision. After that date, they stop receiving their cash support and – in case they were provided accommodation to live as asylum seekers – they have to move out. Refugees, however, can apply for unemployment benefits, housing benefits, and social housing.

[4] De la Rica et al. (2015) provide a recent review of the evidence on immigrants' integration in receiving countries.

although there is mixed evidence on whether refugees ever converge to migrants' outcomes and at what speed.[5]

While a growing body of evidence focused on the effect of immigration on crime in host societies (see previous chapters for references), very few studies have so far tried to empirically asses the involvement of asylum seekers and refugees in criminal activities. In particular, three papers have studied whether the presence of migrants seeking humanitarian protection leads to higher crime rates in hosting societies (in the UK, Germany, and the USA, respectively). Bell et al. (2013) studied the impact of asylum seekers on crime in the UK. Their empirical strategy relies on a dispersal policy whereby asylum applicants are assigned to different local authorities while they wait for their claim to be processed. The assignment to different areas is determined predominantly by availability of spare social housing, and as a result asylum seekers are frequently allocated to relatively disadvantage areas that have experienced reductions in resident population. The dispersal policy is coupled with a six-month ban on legal labour market access for asylum seekers. Bell et al. (2013) found that areas that hosted more 'dispersed' asylum claimants had slightly higher rates of property crime than otherwise similar places, but no substantive difference in rates of violent crime. The effect is driven entirely by differences in the number of male asylum seekers. Bell et al. (2013) suggest that the policy setting asylum seekers face in the UK may generate incentives to engage in crime by harming their labour market integration. Gehrsitz and Ungerer (2017) focused on the recent refugee wave in Germany and analysed short-term effects on labour markets and crime across German counties. Similarly to previous research, they found that refugees struggled to find employment. When looking at crime rates, they found evidence of an increase in crime in areas that hosted

---

[5]   For the USA, evidence of refugees catching up with – and even overtaking – migrants is found by Cortes (2004). In Canada, Bevelander and Pendakur (2014) found that refugees never reach migrants' level of assimilation, although they gradually approach it. Evidence of divergence after the first five years of residence is instead observed by Bratsberg et al. (2017) in Norway.

more refugees. Consistent with Bell et al. (2013), the effect they identified is small – a full standard deviation increase in asylum seekers inflow in one area would imply a 1.5% increase in overall crime rate – and it is driven mainly by an increase in drug offenses and fare-dodging. The US context is studied in Amuedo-Dorantes et al. (2018). The USA uses a resettlement scheme to relocate refugees from transit countries to the USA. Individuals displaced from their home country by conflict, and who have moved into neighbouring countries, can apply for asylum in the USA. If their claim is successful, they are then transferred to the USA and assigned to one of nine resettlement agencies that will then allocate them to a specific municipality. Notably, these resettlement agencies explicitly try to match refugees to areas where they are more likely to be integrated into the local economy, and there are no policy-based limitations on their labour force participation (Dagnelie et al., 2017). Amuedo-Dorantes et al. (2018) exploit variation in the geographical and temporal distribution of refugees across US counties to investigate if there is a significant link between refugee settlements and local crime rates (and terrorist events). Unlike in Europe, their regression analysis fails to uncover any statistically significant evidence of such a relationship. No significant effect is found when the sample is restricted to the seven nationalities included in the travel ban issued by US president Trump in January 2017.[6] The contrasting results in Europe and the USA suggest that labour market opportunities may directly influence the relationship between refugees and local crime rates.

Two other studies have explicitly examined the determinants of refugees' propensity to engage in crime. Damm and Dustmann (2014) analyse whether refugee children who were exposed to higher crime in the municipality of residence at a young age were then

---

[6]   On 27 January 2017, President Trump issued the executive order 'Protecting the Nation from Terrorist Attacks by Foreign Nationals' and mandated a temporary travel ban for citizens from a list of countries (Iran, Iraq, Libya, Somalia, Sudan, Syria, and Yemen) considered being a risk for producing terrorism attacks in the USA.

more likely to be offenders in the future. Their identification relies on a dispersal policy of refugee migrants that was implemented in Denmark between 1986 and 1998 and generated quasi-random variation in assignment to municipalities. They found that refugees who grow up in higher crime places are more likely to offend in the future. Specifically, Damm and Dustmann (2014) found that the share of young people convicted of crimes – violent crimes in particular – in the assigned municipality of residence is positively related to both the probability of receiving a conviction and the number of convictions of male refugee children later in life. The effect is particularly strong for conviction rates of individuals of the same ethnic group, suggesting that social interactions play a key role in linking individual criminal behaviour with area crime. For Switzerland, Couttenier et al. (2016) focus instead on potential differences in propensity to engage in violent crime among asylum seekers. In particular, they show that asylum seekers exposed to violence in the home country during their childhood are significantly more violent than co-nationals who were born after the conflict.[7] Using data on the nationality of both victims and offenders, they further show that individuals who experienced more violence in source countries have a higher propensity to target victims of their same nationality. Couttenier et al. (2016) suggest that exposure to conflict may have permanent effects on individual violent behaviour, and may generate persistent intranational rivalries. Further, after examining variation in public policies across different Swiss cantons, they found that the increased propensity to offence can potentially be mitigated by integration policies. In particular, there is no relationship between exposure to violence and criminal behaviour in cantons offering labour market access to asylum seekers.

---

[7] Note that they do not compare the propensity for engaging in violent crime of asylum seekers with respect to natives or other immigrant populations. Their study, therefore, does not allow drawing any conclusion on the impact of asylum seekers on overall violent crime rates in Switzerland.

5.3 DATA AND DESCRIPTIVE STATISTICS

The empirical analysis developed in this chapter is based on a longitudinal dataset of EU countries that was obtained by merging data from two main sources.

Asylum seekers and refugees. First, we collected UNHCR records on asylum seekers and refugees.[8] Yearly data on refugee population – disaggregated by country of origin – are available since 1990 for all European countries and count the number of individuals who have refugee status and are resident in each country at the end of each year. In addition, we use yearly data on the number asylum applications filed in each country: these data are available since 2000 and can also be disaggregated by country of origin of the applicant.

Descriptive statistics for the UNHCR records in EU15 countries that we use in our empirical analysis are reported in Table A.9.[9] In the first three rows of the table, countries are ranked according to the average number of asylum applications (per 10,000 population) that they received between 2000 and 2015. The EU15 average over this period is 8.7 applications per 10,000 residents filed each year by asylum seekers. Five countries are below this average: Portugal (0.2), Spain (1.3), Italy (4.1), the UK (6.8), and France (7.8). Over the same period, the five EU15 countries that have received the highest number of yearly applications per capita are Sweden (42.9), Austria (29.8), Luxembourg (21.7), Ireland (18.4), and Belgium (17.1). In the last three rows of Table A.9, we focus instead on the refugee population. Between 1995 and 2015, in the EU15 there were on average approximately 40 refugees per 10,000 population. Five countries are above the EU15 average: Sweden (141.8), Germany (94.5), Denmark (84.2), the Netherlands (64.1), and Austria (54.2). These figures are in stark contrast with those of Southern European countries. Over the period we are considering, there were on average just 0.4 refugees for every

---

[8]   See Hatton (2009) and Hatton (2016) for a description and analysis of these UNHCR records.

[9]   All tables discussed in this chapter are provided in Appendix 3.

10,000 residents in Portugal, 1.3 in Spain, 4.7 in Greece, and 7.7 in Italy. Ireland also hosted few refugees: 9.4 per 10,000 population.

Crime rates. Detailed records on national crime rates are collected from Eurostat, our second source of data. Crime data are consistently reported for the period 1995–2015 for the following categories of crime: burglary, robbery, vehicle theft, drug crime, and homicide. Since 2008, data for three additional types of violent offences – assault, rape, and sexual assault – are available. When using cross-country crime data one should be aware that issues of data comparability may arise. Heterogeneity in national definitions of criminal offences, in victims' propensity to report, and in police recording practices may generate differences in levels and trends of recorded crime rates that may be very different from levels and trends in underlying crime rates. These measurement issues are less concerning for extremely serious crimes such as murder, but may complicate the econometric modelling of other serious offences such as rape and sexual assault. We describe how we address this problem in Section 5.5 of this chapter.

In Table A.10, we show average crime rates (i.e. number of offences per 10,000 population) for different types of offences in EU15 countries. The average are computed over the period 1995–2015 for property crime (burglary, robbery, and vehicle theft), drug crime, and homicide. Averages for assault, rape, and sexual assault are computed for the period 2008–15, as these data were not available before 2008. Crimes against property are the most frequent types of criminal offences. On average, approximately thirty-five burglaries, thirty-three vehicle thefts, and thirteen robberies (per 10,000 population) were officially recorded in EU15 countries each year between 1995 and 2015. The official burglary crime rate varies between 15.2 in Finland and 77.2 in Denmark, vehicle theft crime rate between 15.3 (Greece) and 23 (Belgium), and robbery crime rate between 8.1 (Austria) and 61.1 (Sweden), although again these levels of differences do not necessarily imply the actual crime rates vary across countries in this way. Almost 6 drug offences per 10,000 population were recorded on average in the EU15 in this period, reaching a minimum of 1 in France and a maximum of 23.2 in Denmark. Finally, assault is the most frequent offence among violent crimes, with a EU15 yearly average of 27.7 recorded offences per 10,000 residents. The other, more serious, violent offences are instead far less frequent: the average crime rate is 3.2 for sexual assault, 1.4 for rape, and 0.13 for homicide.

5.4 GRAPHICAL ANALYSIS

In this section, we provide a graphical visualization of the correlation between crime rates and asylum seekers' or refugees' flows in selected European countries. In particular, we focus on eight of the major recipient countries of asylum seekers and refugees: Germany, the UK, France, Sweden, the Netherlands, Italy, Austria, and Denmark. An econometric analysis of all EU countries is developed and presented in Section 5.5.

We start our graphical inspection by plotting crime rates over time for selected offences, which we then contrast with the evolution of the asylum seeker and refugee populations. The graphs refer to the period 1995–2016.[10] Trends in property (robbery, burglary, and car theft) and drug crime are reported in Figure 5.3 (countries: FR, DE, SE, UK) and in Figure 5.4 (countries: AT, DK, IT, NL). Homicide rates are reported in Figure 5.5 (countries: FR, DE, SE, UK) and Figure 5.6 (countries: AT, DK, IT, NL). All four figures display the time series of both the refugee population and the number of asylum applications in the respective set of countries.

These graphs highlight the vast heterogeneity observable across EU countries in the exposure to refugee flows. From 1995 to 2016, we can see that some countries – such as France, Austria, and Italy – hosted a growing refugee population. Other countries (Germany, Sweden, Denmark, and the Netherlands) were on a declining trend, one that was partially reversed in 2015 by the latest

---

[10] Records on asylum seeker applications are available only since 2000 (see Section 3).

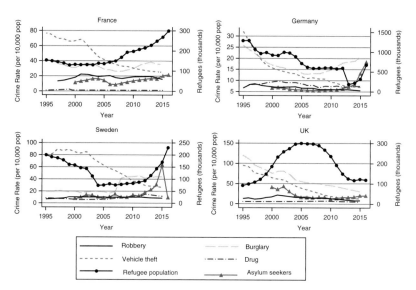

FIGURE 5.3 Property and drug crime: FR, DE, SE, UK, 1995–2016.

Note: The figure reports the time series of selected crime rates (robbery, burglary, vehicle theft, and drug; source: Eurostat), refugee population and number of asylum applications (source: UNHCR). Countries: France, Germany, Sweden, and the UK.

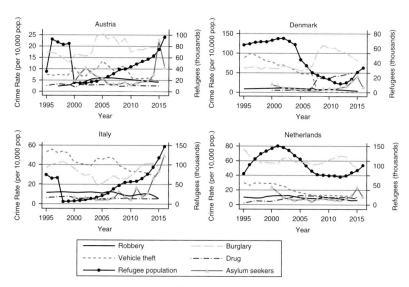

FIGURE 5.4 Property and drug crime: AT, DK, IT, NL, 1995–2016.

Note: The figure reports the time series of selected crime rates (robbery, burglary, vehicle theft, and drug; source: Eurostat), refugee population and number of asylum applications (source: UNHCR). Countries: Austria, Denmark, Italy, and the Netherlands.

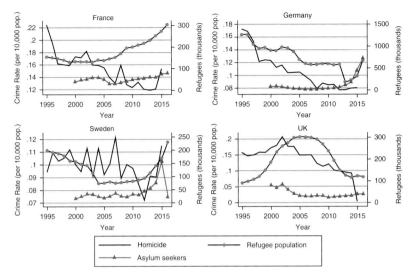

FIGURE 5.5 Homicide rate: FR, DE, SE, UK, 1995–2016.

Note: The figure reports the time series of homicide crime rate (source: Eurostat), refugee population, and number of asylum applications (source: UNHCR). Countries: France, Germany, Sweden, and the UK.

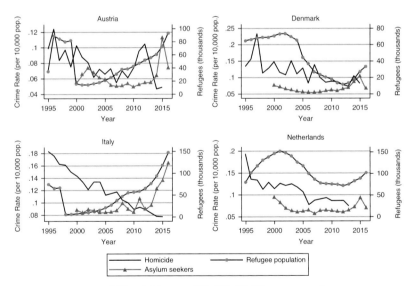

FIGURE 5.6 Homicide rate: AT, DK, IT, NL, 1995–2016.

Note: The figure reports the time series of homicide crime rate (source: Eurostat), refugee population, and number of asylum applications (source: UNHCR). Countries: Austria, Denmark, Italy, and the Netherlands.

refugee crisis.[11] The refugee population in the UK, in contrast to these countries, exhibits a distinct inverted U-shaped trend: it reached a peak in 2006 and experienced a sharp decline since then. In most countries, there is a sudden increase in asylum applications around 2015: the spike is remarkably pronounced in Germany, Sweden, Austria, and Italy and, to a lesser extent, in Denmark and the Netherlands.

A general decline in crime rates is visible in both Figures 5.3 and 5.4, although there exists substantial heterogeneity across countries and criminal offences. At first sight, it is difficult to spot any obvious co-movement in the number of crimes and of individuals seeking humanitarian protection. An upward trend in burglaries is visible in several countries (France, Germany, Sweden, Denmark, and Italy) but it started between 2005 and 2010, hence well before the latest refugee crisis, and can therefore hardly be attributed to any systematic change in the number of refugees or asylum applicants.

Time series for homicide rates for the same set of eight host countries are reported in Figures 5.5 and 5.6. The number of murders shows sizeable year-to-year variation in many countries, but generally follows a downward trend over the last twenty years (with the exception of Austria and Sweden). As for the previous figures, it is hard to recognize any clear correlation between changes in the number of refugees and asylum seekers and the trends in homicide rates across these European countries.

Although informative about overall trends in the main variables of interest for our analysis, time series graphs such as the preceding figures are not perfectly suitable for uncovering correlations between changes in crime rates and changes in the refugee population. Therefore, we also plot yearly changes in crime rates against yearly changes in refugee. These graphs would immediately highlight whether increases in the population of refugees or in the number of

[11]   Note that the sharp drop in refugee population observable in Germany between 2012 and 2013 is due to a harmonization of the definitions used to count refugees (see UNHCR, 2014).

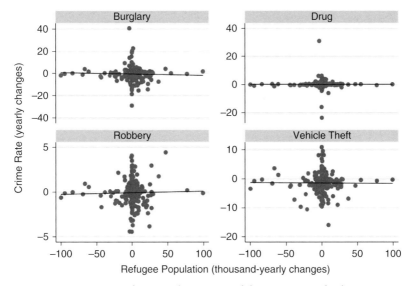

FIGURE 5.7 Refugees and property and drug crime: yearly changes in
EU15 countries, 1995–2015.

Note: The figure reports yearly changes in crime rates (burglary, drug,
robbery, and vehicle theft) on the vertical axis and yearly changes in the
refugee population on the horizontal axis. Each dot in the graph
corresponds to one observation of these yearly changes for one of the EU15
countries included in the sample. The estimated slopes of the fitted lines
are not statistically different from zero.

individuals arriving to seek asylum are associated with positive
changes in crime rates. We consider all EU15 countries' yearly
changes in officially recorded property and drug crime rates (on the
vertical axis) against yearly changes in the refugee population (Figure
5.7) and in asylum applications (Figure 5.8). Each dot in the graph
corresponds to one observation of these yearly changes for one of the
EU15 countries included in the sample. If a larger presence of individuals seeking humanitarian protection – or having refugee status –
was associated with higher crime rates, we would expect to see the
dots scattered around a positively sloped line. The continuous lines
are the linear fits for each scatterplot, which are obtained by inter-
polating a straight line through the points in the graph. The lines are
generally flat, irrespective of the variable used to measure the presence

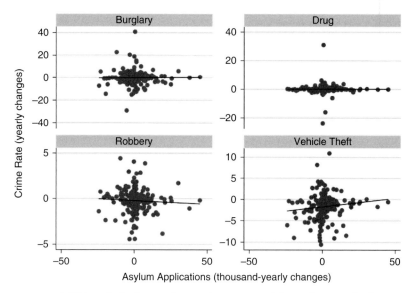

FIGURE 5.8 Asylum seekers and property and drug crime: yearly changes in EU15 countries, 1995–2015.

Note: The figure reports yearly changes in crime rates (burglary, drug, robbery, and vehicle theft) on the vertical axis and yearly changes in the number of asylum applications on the horizontal axis. Each dot corresponds to one observation of these yearly changes for one of the EU15 countries included in the sample. The estimated slopes of the fitted lines are not statistically different from zero (the slope for vehicle theft is only marginally significant).

of refugees in the host country. This flatness suggests the absence of a significant (unconditional) correlation between crime and refugees. The only exception is the positive slop of the relationship between changes in vehicle theft crime and changes in asylum applicants.

Graphs of violent crime do not appear to be substantially different from those of property offences. In addition to homicide rates, of which records are available for the entire period 1995–2015, we can also look at assault, rape, and sexual assault; crime rates for these additional violent offences are available since 2008. Scatterplots of yearly changes in violent crime rates versus yearly changes in refugee population and asylum applications are reported

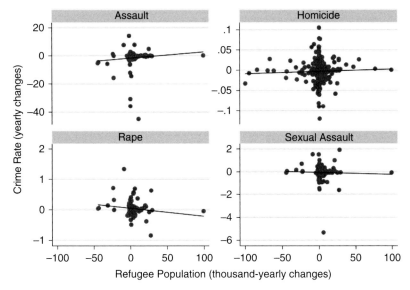

FIGURE 5.9 Refugees and violent crime: yearly changes in EU15 countries, 1995–2015.

Note: The figure reports yearly changes in crime rates (assault, homicide, rape, and sexual assault) on the vertical axis and yearly changes in the refugee population on the horizontal axis. Each dot corresponds to one observation of these yearly changes for one of the EU15 countries included in the sample. The estimated slopes of the fitted lines are not statistically different from zero. Crime data for assault, rape, and sexual assault are available only for the period 2008–2015.

in Figures 5.9 and 5.10, respectively. As these figures illustrate, we fail to find any strong correlation between changes in violent crime rates and changes in the population of refugees or asylum seekers. In Figure 5.9, the fitted lines suggest a positive correlation between assault and number of refugees, while the relation is negative for rape, a finding in direct contrast to a much publicized 2015/2016 incident of alleged sexual assaults committed by suspected North African refugees on New Year's Eve in Cologne, Germany.[12]

12   See, for instance, *The Economist* (9 January 2016) 'New Year, New Fear'; www.econ omist.com/news/europe/21685512-attacks-women-mobs-young-men-inflame-germa nys-refugee-debate-new-year-new-fear

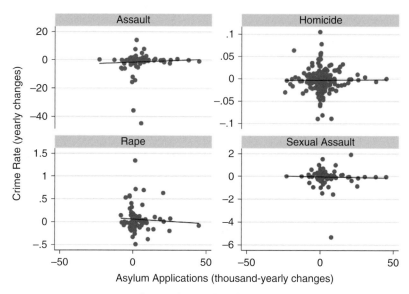

FIGURE 5.10 Asylum seekers and violent crime: yearly changes in EU15 countries, 1995–2015.

Note: The figure reports yearly changes in crime rates (assault, homicide, rape, and sexual assault) on the vertical axis and yearly changes in the number of asylum applications on the horizontal axis. Each dot corresponds to one observation of these yearly changes for one of the EU15 countries included in the sample. The estimated slopes of the fitted lines are not statistically different from zero (the slope for vehicle theft is only marginally significant). Crime data for assault, rape, and sexual assault are available only for the period 2008–15.

Further, both lines become flatter in Figure 5.10, when we look at asylum application rather than refugee population.

5.5   EMPIRICAL STRATEGY

The graphical evidence of the previous section has some limitations. The most important one is that it does not control for other changes in the country that may influence both the trends in immigration and in crime. For example, a country with a growing economy might increase its numbers of refugees and asylum seekers and, at the same time, see its crime rates drop as more and more people find good jobs. For this reason, we are going to use an econometric model that allows us to hold fixed all those variables that might interfere with the relationship between refugees and crime. In our empirical analysis, we estimate first differences (FD) panel regression of crime rates and refugee populations in EU countries. This means that we test whether yearly changes in the refugee population residing in one country affect yearly changes in national crime rates, controlling for changes in other variables that may also influence crime. In particular, our estimating equation is the following:

$$\Delta \ln \left(\frac{\text{crime}_{rt}}{\text{pop}_{rt}} \right) = \beta \Delta \ln \left(\frac{\text{ref}_{rt}}{\text{pop}_{rt}} \right) + \gamma \Delta X_{rt} + \theta_t + \varepsilon_{rt} \tag{5.1}$$

where: $\ln \left(\frac{\text{crime}_{rt}}{\text{pop}_{rt}} \right)$ is the log crime rate (number of offences per 10,000 population) recorded in country r in year t and $\ln \left(\frac{\text{ref}_{rt}}{\text{pop}_{rt}} \right)$ is the log of the share of refugees/asylum seekers over total population residing in country r in year t. Throughout our empirical analysis, we define the variable $\ln \left(\frac{\text{ref}_{rt}}{\text{pop}_{rt}} \right)$ in two ways: the number of refugees residing in a country in a given year and, alternatively, the number of asylum applications yearly received by the country. In both cases, we normalize the variable by dividing it by the resident population. Our specification further includes a vector X_{rt} of time variant country level controls (log total population, log GDP per capita, youth unemployment rate, share of population aged 15 to 24, and share of population with low education); θ_t are year dummies that capture any common European trend; ε_{rt} is an idiosyncratic shock. The Δ operator means that, for each variable, we are taking the difference between the values in the current year (t) and in the previous year ($t-1$).

Unobserved country effects may potentially be correlated with both the levels of crime and the number of refugees hosted or asylum applications submitted in any given country. For example, it might well be that refugees seek out countries with better legal systems, but these might also be countries whose crimes rates tend to be lower. Alternatively, individuals seeking humanitarian protection may prefer wealthier countries in which they may expect to receive more generous asylum support. If richer countries have lower crime rates we may expect to observe a negative correlation between crime and the size of the refugee population. We address this concern by using an FD estimator that removes any persistent time-invariant unobservable fixed effect (e.g. legal systems) that may potentially bias our estimates. Our empirical analysis therefore exploits within-country variation in crime and refugees (asylum seekers) population and investigates whether a significant correlation between these two variables can be uncovered in the data.

Note that the use of an FD estimator partially addresses previously mentioned concerns about cross-country variation in crime reporting standards. Any constant country-level difference in the definition of or propensity to report crime will be taken out of our analysis by the FDs. Our only necessary assumption is that any changes in propensity to report are not correlated with changes in the number of refugees and asylum seekers. It is not only variation in reporting standards that are of concern; it is not difficult to think of situations in which other unobserved shocks might induce a spurious correlation between refugees and actual crime. For example, a country that enters a recession may experience both an increase in crime rates and a reduction in the number of individuals arriving to seek asylum (Cadena and Kovak, 2016). As mentioned, the inclusion in our regressions of time varying socio-economic controls – GDP per capita, youth unemployment rate, share of young population, etc. – precisely aims at capturing these potential shocks.[13]

[13] In this chapter, we do not develop an instrumental variable strategy to address any other residual endogeneity concern. We must therefore be cautious in giving a causal interpretation to our estimates. Notwithstanding, we would argue that, conditional on our set of controls, most of the within-country variation in asylum applications and refugees we exploit is driven by conflict and other push factors in source countries combined with the geographical proximity of potential destination countries. Under this assumption, the variation we use is (mostly) exogenous in our regressions.

5.6 RESULTS

In this section, we present our estimates of the elasticity of crime rates with respect to the number of refugees and asylum seekers. We first focus on EU15 countries and consider different types of criminal offences: property, drug, and violent crime. Further, we study the timing of the effect. We conclude by reporting estimates for the New Member States (NMS) of the EU.

Property and drug crime. Table A.11 reports our estimates of the impact of changes in the refugee population on three types of property crime (burglary, robbery and vehicle theft; see panel A) and on drug crime (panel B). We exclusively report the estimates for the β coefficient in Eq. (5.1), namely the elasticity of crime with respect to the presence of refugees or asylum seekers in the country. The sample includes EU15 countries over the period 1995–2015. For each criminal offence, we start with a baseline specification that includes only year dummies (column 1) and we then gradually add country-level controls. Column 5 reports estimates obtained with the most restrictive specification that controls for log total population, log GDP per capita, youth unemployment rate, share of population aged 15 to 24, and share of population with low education. In all regressions, standard errors are clustered at the country level to allow for any within-country serial correlation in shocks.

The estimates in Table A.11 suggest that increases in the refugee population hosted in EU countries are not statistically associated with increases in property or drug crime rates. If anything, the negative and statistically significant coefficients we find for burglary and robbery (see Panel A, columns 1–4) would suggest the opposite for these two specific criminal offences. In both cases, however, the coefficients lose their statistical significance in column 5, when we include all the country controls (and we have a smaller sample size). Coefficients for vehicle theft and drug are instead not statistically different from zero in all specifications. Similar conclusions can be reached by looking at Table A.12. The structure of the table and the specifications are as in Table A.11, but we now replace yearly changes in the refugee population with yearly changes in the number of asylum applications received by each country in the sample. We fail to uncover any significant correlation between property and drug crime rates and asylum applicants.

Violent crime. Estimates of the elasticity of violent crime with respect to the refugee population and in the number of asylum applicants are reported in Table A.13 and A.14, respectively. Four types of violent crime are considered: assault, homicide, rape, and sexual assault.[14] As in the previous two tables, we report unconditional estimates in column 1 and we then gradually add country controls to the specification. Both Tables A.13 and A.14 clearly point at the absence of any statistically significant association between increases in the size of populations seeking humanitarian protection and the incidence of criminal acts that involve violence against individuals. In the two tables taken together, we find only one significant coefficient (on rape; column 4 in Table A.14) but it actually suggests that more refugees are associated with fewer, not more, rapes.

Timing of the effect. The estimates reported so far would imply the lack of a contemporaneous impact of asylum seekers and refugees on crime rates in receiving societies. As a matter of fact, it is still possible that changes in the size of the populations seeking humanitarian protection do affect crime, but that change happens slowly, rather than in the first year of the immigrants' arrival. In Tables A.15 and A.16, we investigate the timing of this potential effect. In Table A.15 we focus on changes in the refugee population and we consider both property and drug crime (panel A) and violent crime (panel B). In odd columns, we include both the contemporaneous change in the (log) refugee population and its first lag, meaning the change that happened a year earlier. In even columns, we condition only on the first lag. We

[14] Data for assault, rape, and sexual assault are available only since 2008. See Section 3 on data description.

include controls for the full set of country regressors in all columns. This new set of estimates confirms our previous findings. Even if we allow for a lag in the effect, we fail to find any evidence of a significant impact of refugees on crime rates. Table A.16 replicates the same empirical exercise but uses changes in the number of asylum applications rather than in the refugee population. Estimates are still not significantly different from zero.

New Member States (NMS13). All estimates that we have discussed so far refer to a sample of EU15 countries. One potential reason that we do not find that hosting more refugees or asylum seekers is associated with higher crime rates may be that EU15 countries have a long-lasting experience in hosting refugees, and have therefore developed asylum policies that are effective in avoiding their marginalization. Our findings may be very different when looking at NMS of the European Union (NMS13) that are poorer and relatively less experienced in managing flows of asylum seekers. We empirically investigate this conjecture in Table A.17, where we replicate our previous analysis for a sample of NMS13 countries. Panels A and B focus on changes in the refugee population and in the number of asylum seeker applications, respectively. In both panels, we look at all types of criminal offences we have studied so far. Estimates reported in odd columns only control for year dummies while in even columns we condition on the full set of country controls. Our findings for NMS13 countries are remarkably similar to those discussed for EU15 countries. The ?estimated coefficients in Table A.17 show that even in the context of NMS13 countries the arrival of asylum seekers and the presence of refugees is not systematically correlated with higher crime rates.

5.7   CONCLUDING REMARKS

In this chapter, we examined the question of whether or not EU countries that received larger inflows of people seeking humanitarian protection experienced statistically significant increases in their crime rates. After merging UNHCR records on asylum seekers with

Eurostat data on crime rates for different types of offences, we construct a panel dataset for all EU countries that cover the period from 1995 to 2016.

We began with a visual inspection of these data, plotting time series of our main variables of interest and producing scatterplots that contrast within-country changes in crime with within-country changes in asylum applications and in refugee population. These graphs did not reveal a clear correlation between the presence of refugees and higher crime rates. We further investigated this possibility by developing a rigorous econometric analysis. We estimate first differences panel regressions of crime on asylum applications and refugees. These regressions allowed us to remove any permanent differences across countries that may contemporaneously be correlated with both the level of crime and the size of the refugee population. Moreover, we also controlled for a set of main country regressors (total population, log GDP per capita, youth unemployment rate, etc.) that are also likely to be correlated with both our dependent and our main independent variables. Although we cannot claim that our estimates identify a purely causal parameter, the results from all our regressions strongly point at the lack of a statistically significant impact of refugee migrants on crime rates in EU15 countries. Irrespective of the measure of refugee migration we use – asylum applications or total refugee population – we fail to find a significant impact on any of the eight categories of criminal offences we consider (burglary, robbery, vehicle theft, drug, assault, homicide, rape, and sexual assault) in our analysis. Allowing the effect to appear with some lag also leads to insignificant estimates. Finally, using the sample of NMS13 countries rather than EU15 countries does not change our findings.

The empirical analysis we develop in this chapter casts doubt on the conjecture that a larger presence of refugees should be necessarily associated to rising crime rates. As a matter of fact, the evidence we present on the EU countries' experience between 1995 and 2016 is compatible with the absence of any such effect, at least at the aggregate level. Our country-level analysis, however, does not allow to uncover potential local effects. Within each hosting country, the spatial distribution of asylum seekers and refugees is typically not even across areas. If locations that host relatively more refugees experience increases in crime – and if these increases are not large enough as to shift national crime rates or are accompanied by reductions elsewhere – we would not see any effect in the country data we are using. The current refugee crisis offers a unique setting to better investigate these spatial effects in future research.

Conclusion

Few policy issues generate as much heated rhetoric and embroiled debate as immigration regulation. Who should be allowed to transverse a border and become a citizen? What restrictions, if any, should a government place on the economic and social activity of migrants? In this book, we documented the varying approaches that governments in different parts of the world, and at different points in time, have approached this question. In doing so, we have focused our attention on one motivation, and outcome, of immigration policy: the criminal behaviour of immigrants.

Our motivation for focusing on crime and public safety is based on what people say matters to them. We show that while, as a matter of fact, the relationship between immigration and crime is deeply ambiguous, public attitudes about immigration are tightly linked to fears that immigrants, particularly undocumented immigrants, will bring with them increases in crime. This fear of the criminal immigrant is evident in both transnational surveys and the historic record of immigration policy in the USA.

What we point out is that, while we generally fail to find evidence that immigrants, on average, commit substantially more crime than native-born residents of similar age and position, economic theory identifies several mechanisms through which immigration policy itself can either cause, or mitigate, criminal behaviour by immigrants. Most strikingly, we document a relationship between the ability of immigrants to work in the formal sector and their criminal behaviour, which is surprisingly consistent in the UK, in Italy, and in the USA. Any policymaker, or voter, interested in the criminal behaviour of immigrants should take notice of this; unlike age, gender, or previous education, the legal work status of immigrants is entirely within the control of the destination country. If the goal is to reduce the number of crimes committed by immigrants, sound empirical evidence says that policymakers should encourage, rather than discourage, immigrants to enter the labour force.

We base this conclusion on multiple pieces of evidence. First, we study how the Italian government has regulated immigration. Italy generally restricts the ability of non-Italians to enter the country and work through annual 'Flows Decrees', which set quotas for the number of people from each country allowed to enter. Any immigrants who enter the country after a given quota is met are considered irregular. However, the government periodically issues large-scale amnesties that allow irregular immigrants to declare themselves present in Italy, and with few conditions become eligible to 'regularize' themselves. We show that immigrants in general, and irregular immigrants in particular, appear to be over-represented in Italian prisons, but in the years immediately following these amnesties, the foreign-born population in Italian prisons drops substantially.

This population level phenomenon, in which the expansion of legal status is followed by a reduction in the rate at which immigrants commit crime, is replicated at the individual level. In addition to periodic amnesties, Pinotti (2017) documents a second path to legal status in Italy, the internet-based 'click days'. Pinotti (2017) shows clear evidence that individuals who miss the cutoff for 'click day' legal status are more likely to be rearrested than individuals who managed to submit their application literally fractions of a second before. In this case, the granting of legal status is mathematically equivalent to an experiment that randomly allows some immigrants the ability to work in the formal sector, and the clear result is a reduction in their criminal behaviour.

We then turn to the UK, which has had a longer history of receiving large waves of immigrants than Italy. That said, we document a relatively recent shift in the composition of immigrants, as well as a general increase in the net rate of immigration (which takes into account the rate at which people leave the UK). In particular, we show that prison statistics suggest that immigrants from 'New Member' EU states – Bulgaria, Croatia, Cyprus, Czech Republic, Estonia, Hungary, Latvia, Lithuania, Malta, Poland, Romania, Slovakia, and Slovenia – have become increasingly involved in UK crime.

With this in mind, we then examine whether or not the increase in number of immigrants from these new countries could be driving crime rates across the UK. We do this by comparing the violent, property, and drug offences in regions where the foreign-born population is rising faster to regions where the foreign-born population is growing more slowly, or even falling. What we observe is that there is generally no data-driven relationship between the rate at which people from outside the UK move to an area and the incidence of crime.

However, when we allow the relationship between immigration and crime to vary with economic conditions, a different picture emerges. Specifically, after the Great Recession, we do find a more positive relationship between changes in the foreign-born population and crime rates. The finding that immigration may increase crime during a recession is consistent with existing evidence on the UK immigrant experience. Specifically, Bell et al. (2013) document that local increases in the population of immigrants who are allowed to live in the UK, but legally prohibited from working, are associated with increases in property offences. Other research on immigration and crime in the UK, which does not specifically look at the population of immigrants who are unable to work, generally finds that immigration either reduces (Bell and Machin, 2013), or is unrelated (Jaitman and Machin, 2013) to local crime rates. While the assumptions necessary for a causal interpretation are perhaps stronger than the research in Italy, the pattern of findings across different studies suggests that the ability of immigrants to find legal jobs determines whether or not those immigrants will participate in crime.

Across the Atlantic, immigration policy in the USA has gone through many iterations, commonly divided into 'Open Door', 'Door Ajar', 'Pet Door', and 'Dutch Door' periods. We build on these historical divisions to differentiate between ex ante immigration policies that restrict who is allowed to enter the USA and ex post policies that restrict what immigrants are allowed to do after they arrive.

In spite of the fact that debates about immigration policy have frequently focused on the criminality of immigrants, we show that there is only scant evidence that the immigrants portrayed as immoral or dangerous actually were. For example, for most of US history, immigrants from Asian countries were characterized as particularly dangerous, in spite of the fact that, once settlement patterns are taken into account, Asian people were generally much less likely to be incarcerated than natives. In contrast, immigrants from Mexico were somewhat over-represented in prisons, but until the 1940s were given somewhat preferential treatment in ex post immigration regulations.

One example of ex post immigration policy favouring immigrants from Mexico is the 1917 Literacy Act, which required immigrants to be able to read in any language as a condition of entry. Mexican immigrants who were entering the country to work in agriculture were exempt from this requirement. Using Census data on the timing of immigration and incarceration, we show that the 1917 Act altered the composition of the immigrant population to one that was actually more literate than natives. Consistent with this, we find that the human-capital–based ex post restriction on immigration is associated with a reduction in the number of immigrants behind bars.

We then describe what, until the recent past, was arguably one of the larger 'shocks' to US immigration policy, the Immigration Reform and Control Act (IRCA) of 1986. One of the enduring legacies of IRCA was the granting of amnesty to almost 3 million people who were living and working in the USA without proper documentation. Recent research has identified three different links between this amnesty program and crime. First, Baker (2015) presents evidence that places where more immigrants eventually gained full citizenship also experienced reductions in crime. Comino et al. (2016) document another interesting aspect of the immigrant policy–crime relationship: how do crime victims respond to immigration policy? They present evidence that crime victims who became citizens through IRCA are more likely to notify the police. Second, Freedman et al. (2018) document that, similar to the Italian 'click days' experiment, the end of the amnesty application period was associated with a relative increase in the criminal behaviour of new immigrants. Both of these changes in the integration of immigrants into society support an economic interpretation of the immigration–crime link; policies that allow immigrants to participate fully in society (i.e. citizenship) result in less criminal behaviour by immigrants. Policies that limit the ability of immigrants to work (i.e. terminating their ability to receive temporary visitor status) cause the immigrant crime rate to go up.

Finally, we turn from a destination country-based analysis of immigration policy to a source-country one. Recent political upheaval and extraordinary violence in some parts of the world has led to a spike in refugees and asylum seekers in the EU and USA. And, as we have documented in both US and EU history, this shift in the composition of immigrants has coincided with increased public fears of the criminality of the new, different, arrivals. After reviewing the existing research, and conducting our own cross-country analysis of the refugee and asylum seeking and crime rates, we identify further evidence supporting our hypothesis. The criminality of immigrants is not preordained but, rather, government policy plays a central role in whether or not the 'immigrant other' is actually manifest. Specifically, refugees who are exposed to high levels of violence are more likely to offend in their destination countries, but government programs aimed at integrating these 'involuntary migrants' into society, including the labour market, appear to mitigate this relationship. Cross-country variation in the labour market access that refugees have is a potential explanation for our finding that, on average, there is no statistically significant, empirical connection between the arrival of refugees or asylum seekers and serious crimes.

History provides almost no examples of a country being able to successfully 'close' its borders; the ability of people to circumvent physical or legal barriers to immigration may be limitable, but is clearly not stoppable. To some extent, public fear about the morality or criminality of immigrants, particularly when those immigrants are culturally dissimilar from natives, is not easily legislated away. We have argued in this book that those two ideas do not have to be in conflict. In fact, the criminal behaviour of immigrants appears to be very responsive to immigration policy; data on crime, criminal justice involvement, and public policy have repeatedly shown that allowing immigrants to work appears to cause them to offend less. Restricting the ability of immigrants to find legal jobs leads them to commit crime. This relationship appears to hold in different countries and at different times, and unlike the composition or size of the immigrant population, is always entirely at the discretion of government leaders.

APPENDIX 1: Italian Legislation on Immigration

The first attempt at defining an extensive framework to regulate migration and to shape Italian migration policy was made in 1990, after more than a decade of increased migrant inflows. Prior to 1990, the regulation of entrance and distribution of residence permits for foreigners was regulated by the so called 'Codice Rocco', a royal decree issued in 1931. A marginal intervention and the first amnesty occurred in 1986, applying an International Labour Organization convention (no. 143, 1975) aimed at establishing the principle of equality of treatment between foreign and native workers. Four years later, the 'Martelli law' (39/1990) established new rules and tried to introduce a 'planned number' of new entrants each year. As a matter of fact, this number was never fixed and it remained equal to zero, while the immigrants kept entering the country from the 'back door', either by passing the borders irregularly or by overstaying their tourist visas. A second amnesty corresponded to the Martelli law.

The following years were dominated by the political crisis of Albania (1990 and 1997) and the former Yugoslavia (1995, Bosnian war, and 1997, Kosovo war) that produced huge flows of refugees reaching the near Italian coasts. The government response was that of emergency legislation and ad hoc interventions, with a new amnesty process opened in 1995.

In 1998, under the pressure of the commitment to the Schengen Convention, a left-wing government passed the 'Turco–Napolitano law" no. 40/1998 (later confirmed by the Single Act no. 286 of 25 July 1998), in which the Italian migration policy was extensively defined in every single aspect, from the discipline of entry, residence and working conditions, to that of deportations and control of the illegal phenomenon. Apart from a new emphasis on the need to curb undocumented immigration, the main innovation was an effective introduction of a 'programmed entries' system of foreign workers via quotas to be established yearly. At the same time the fourth amnesty was approved.

In 2002, the previous legislation was modified by the 'Bossi–Fini law' (no. 189/2002). Passed by the current right-wing government coalition, its main declared target was increasing the effectiveness of the enforcement against irregular immigration. The same intervention opened the fifth, and last, legalization process.

APPENDIX 2: Appendix Tables – Immigration and Crime in the United Kingdom (chapter 3)

Table A.1 *Countries of origin in 2000 and 2017*

	Year 2000			Year 2017		
Ranking	Countries	No. (thousands)	Share	Countries	No. (thousands)	Share
1	Republic of Ireland	495	0.11	Poland	922	0.10
2	India	433	0.10	India	829	0.09
3	Pakistan	271	0.06	Pakistan	522	0.06
4	Germany	231	0.05	Romania	390	0.04
5	Bangladesh	174	0.04	Republic of Ireland	390	0.04
6	USA	147	0.03	Germany	318	0.03
7	Kenya	138	0.03	Bangladesh	263	0.03
8	Jamaica	128	0.03	Italy	232	0.02
9	South Africa	119	0.03	South Africa	228	0.02
10	Australia	101	0.02	China	216	0.02
11	China	96	0.02	Nigeria	194	0.02
12	Italy	94	0.02	Lithuania	178	0.02
13	France	91	0.02	France	175	0.02
14	Cyprus (EU)	71	0.02	Spain	156	0.02
15	Sri Lanka	69	0.02	USA	153	0.02
Total foreign born		4,423			9,382	

Source: Authors' calculations based on UK Office for National Statistics data.

Table A.2 *Foreign national inmates by area of origin in 2002 and 2016*

	2002		2016		% change
	No.	%	No.	%	2002–16
Africa	1,286	16.7	1,901	19.2	47.8
Asia	881	11.4	1,619	16.4	83.8
Latin America	236	3.1	125	1.3	–47.1
Europe	2,239	29.0	4,999	50.5	123.3
Middle East	179	2.3	484	4.9	169.9
North America	105	1.4	67	0.7	–36.1
Oceania	43	0.6	22	0.2	–49.4
West Indies	2,739	35.5	674	6.8	–75.4
Total	7,709	100.0	9,891	100.0	28.3

Source: Authors' calculations based on Ministry of Justice data.

Table A.3 *European inmates: top ten nationalities in 2002 and 2016*

Ranking	Country	Year 2002		Country	Year 2016	
		No.	Share		No.	Share
1	Irish Republic	662	0.30	Poland	1,012	0.20
2	Turkey	217	0.10	Irish Republic	745	0.15
3	Netherlands	206	0.05	Romania	674	0.13
4	Spain	116	0.05	Albania	512	0.10
5	Serbia	111	0.05	Lithuania	464	0.09
6	Italy	106	0.05	Portugal	236	0.05
7	Germany	100	0.04	Netherlands	170	0.03
8	France	95	0.04	Latvia	146	0.03
9	Portugal	95	0.04	Italy	118	0.02
10	Albania	71	0.03	Slovakia	101	0.02
	Other	460	0.21	Other	821	0.16
	Total	2,239		Total	4,999	

Source: Authors' calculations based on Ministry of Justice data.

Table A.4 *Descriptive statistics*

	Mean	Std. dev.	Min.	Max.	No. of observations
Crime rates					
Property	507.7	220.0	141.1	2,298.7	3,018
Violent	147.4	66.5	36.1	452.2	3,018
Drug	34.5	25.6	4.2	302.2	3,018
Other	39.4	20.9	5.9	156.3	3,018
Immigrant share					
Share of foreign born	10.5	10.2	0.8	58.3	3,018
Share of foreign nationals	6.8	6.7	0.6	38.1	2,866
Other Local Authorities controls					
Resident population	166,373.5	10,7771.4	34,600.0	1,101,400.0	3,018
Employment rate	72.6	5.7	53.3	88.0	3,018
Share of males aged 16–24	5.7	1.2	3.9	12.3	3,018

Source: Authors' calculations based on UK Office for National Statistics and Home Office data.

Table A.5 *Log crime rate and share of foreign-born population – first differences estimates*

	(1)	(2)	(3)	(4)	(5)
	Panel A: Property crime				
Share of foreign born	-0.000	-0.000	-0.000	-0.000	-0.000
	[0.001]	[0.001]	[0.001]	[0.001]	[0.001]
	Panel B: Violent crime				
Share of foreign born	-0.000	-0.000	-0.000	-0.000	-0.000
	[0.001]	[0.001]	[0.001]	[0.001]	[0.001]
	Panel C: Drug crime				
Share of foreign born	0.003	0.003	0.003	0.003	0.003
	[0.002]	[0.002]	[0.002]	[0.002]	[0.002]
	Panel D: Other crime				
Share of foreign born	-0.001	-0.001	-0.001	-0.001	-0.001
	[0.002]	[0.002]	[0.002]	[0.002]	[0.002]
Year dummies	X	X	X	X	X
Log resident population		X	X	X	X
Employment rate			X	X	X
Share of males aged 16–24				X	X
Police force area trends					X
Observations	3,018	3,018	3,018	3,018	3,018

Note: The table reports first-difference estimates of log crime rate on immigrant share in the Local Authority (LA) and other controls. Each panel reports results for a different macro-category of crime. Standard errors are clustered at the LA level.

Table A.6 *Log crime rate and share of foreign nationals – first differences estimates*

	(1)	(2)	(3)	(4)	(5)
			Panel A: Property crime		
Share of foreign born	-0.001	-0.001	-0.001	-0.001	-0.001
	[0.001]	[0.001]	[0.001]	[0.001]	[0.001]
			Panel B: Violent crime		
Share of foreign born	0.001	0.001	0.001	0.001	0.001
	[0.001]	[0.001]	[0.001]	[0.001]	[0.001]
			Panel C: Drug crime		
Share of foreign born	0.003	0.003	0.003	0.003	0.003
	[0.002]	[0.002]	[0.002]	[0.002]	[0.002]
			Panel D: Other crime		
Share of foreign born	-0.001	-0.001	-0.001	-0.001	-0.001
	[0.002]	[0.002]	[0.002]	[0.002]	[0.002]
Year dummies	X	X	X	X	X
Log resident population		X	X	X	X
Employment rate			X	X	X
Share of males aged 16–24				X	X
Police force area trends					X
Observations	2,779	2,779	2,779	2,779	2,779

Note: The table reports first-difference estimates of log crime rate on immigrant share in the Local Authority (LA) and other controls. Each panel reports results for a different macro-category of crime. Standard errors are clustered at the LA level.

Table A.7 *Log crime rate and share of foreign-born population: before and after the 2008 financial crisis – first differences estimates*

	(1)	(2)	(3)	(4)	(5)
			Panel A: Property crime		
Share of foreign born	−0.002**	−0.002**	−0.002**	−0.002**	−0.002**
	[0.001]	[0.001]	[0.001]	[0.001]	[0.001]
Share of foreign born * post2008	0.002***	0.002***	0.002***	0.002***	0.002***
	[0.000]	[0.000]	[0.000]	[0.000]	[0.000]
			Panel B: Violent crime		
Share of foreign born	−0.001	−0.001	−0.001	−0.001	−0.001
	[0.001]	[0.001]	[0.001]	[0.001]	[0.001]
Share of foreign born * post2008	0.001*	0.001**	0.001**	0.001**	0.001**
	[0.000]	[0.000]	[0.000]	[0.000]	[0.000]
			Panel C: Drug crime		
Share of foreign born	0.005**	0.005**	0.005**	0.005**	0.005**
	[0.002]	[0.002]	[0.002]	[0.002]	[0.002]
Share of foreign born * post2008	−0.004***	−0.003***	−0.003***	−0.003***	−0.004***
	[0.001]	[0.001]	[0.001]	[0.001]	[0.001]

Table A.7 (cont.)

	(1)	(2)	(3)	(4)	(5)
			Panel D: Other crime		
Share of foreign born	-0.002	-0.002	-0.002	-0.002	-0.002
	[0.002]	[0.002]	[0.002]	[0.002]	[0.002]
Share of foreign born * post2008	0.002**	0.002**	0.002**	0.001**	0.001**
	[0.001]	[0.001]	[0.001]	[0.001]	[0.001]
Year dummies	X	X	X	X	X
Log resident population		X	X	X	X
Employment rate			X	X	X
Share of males aged 16–24				X	X
Police force area trends					X
Observations	2,779	2,779	2,779	2,779	2,779

Note: The table reports first-difference estimates of log crime rate on immigrant share in the Local Authority (LA) and other controls. Each panel reports results for a different macro-category of crime. Standard errors are clustered at the LA level.
*p < 0.1; **p < 0.05; ***p < 0.01.

Table A.8 *Log crime rate and share of foreign-born population – instrumental variable estimates*

	(1)	(2)	(3)	(4)	(5)
	Panel A: Property crime				
Share of foreign born	-0.004	0.001	0.001	0.002	-0.027
	[0.005]	[0.009]	[0.009]	[0.007]	[0.020]
	Panel B: Violent crime				
Share of foreign born	-0.014**	-0.008	-0.008	-0.009	0.022
	[0.007]	[0.011]	[0.011]	[0.009]	[0.017]
	Panel C: Drug crime				
Share of foreign born	-0.005	0.036	0.036	0.025	0.057
	[0.019]	[0.030]	[0.030]	[0.025]	[0.041]
	Panel D: Other crime				
Share of foreign born	0.046***	0.077**	0.075**	0.052**	-0.002
	[0.016]	[0.032]	[0.031]	[0.022]	[0.029]
Year dummies	X	X	X	X	X
Log resident population		X	X	X	X
Employment rate			X	X	X
Share of males aged 16–24				X	X
Police force area trends					X
Observations	3,018	3,018	3,018	3,018	3,018
IV : F-statistic	17.82	8.99	9.01	12.00	2.80

Note: The table reports IV estimates of log crime rate on immigrant share in the Local Authority (LA) and other controls. The immigrant share is instrumented with the 'supply-push component' instrument. Each panel reports results for a different macro-category of crime. Standard errors are clustered at the LA level.

* $p < 0.1$; ** $p < 0.05$; *** $p < 0.01$.

APPENDIX 3: **Appendix Tables –
Refugee Waves and
Crime: Evidence from
EU Countries
(Chapter 5)**

Table A.9 *Asylum applications and refugee population (per 10,000 population) in EU15 countries*

Country	Asylum applications (per 10,000 pop.)		Country	Asylum applications (per 10,000 pop.)	
	Avg.	Std. dev.		Avg.	Std. dev.
Sweden	42.91	34.77	Sweden	141.78	53.96
Austria	29.79	21.40	Germany	94.50	39.49
Luxembourg	21.74	12.21	Denmark	84.23	46.11
Ireland	18.43	9.06	Netherlands	64.09	19.26
Belgium	17.08	6.50	Austria	54.16	31.58
Denmark	11.68	9.35	EU15	40.18	—
Netherlands	11.23	7.03	Luxembourg	33.45	19.17
Germany	10.08	12.85	UK	32.42	13.46
Greece	9.94	5.01	France	27.29	6.07
Finland	9.13	11.97	Finland	20.48	4.01
EU15	8.67	—	Belgium	17.62	5.63
France	7.76	1.79	Ireland	9.40	7.63
UK	6.81	3.56	Italy	7.75	5.42
Italy	4.07	3.48	Greece	4.71	4.65
Spain	1.35	0.70	Spain	1.28	0.29
Portugal	0.16	0.08	Portugal	0.40	0.13
Years	2000–15			1995–2015	

Note: The table reports the average and the standard deviation of the number of asylum applications (per 10,000 population; period: 2000–2015) and the number of refugees (per 10,000 population; period: 1995–2015) in EU15 countries. Countries are ranked in decreasing order according to the number of asylum application and the size of the refugee population.

Table A.10 *Average crime rates in EU15 countries, by type of offence*

Country	Property crime				Assault	Violent crime		
	Burglary	Robbery	Vehicle theft	Drug crime		Homicide	Rape	Sexual assault
Austria	18.95	4.63	8.11	2.76	4.51	0.08	1.31	3.20
Belgium	63.39	23.04	24.40	11.87	67.27	0.21	2.93	7.01
Denmark	77.21	8.27	46.55	23.23	4.66	0.12	1.63	1.78
Finland	15.20	3.55	32.58	15.37	3.52	0.24	1.73	3.41
France	33.58	18.15	49.02	1.07	34.86	0.16	1.68	2.39
Germany	17.69	6.72	14.88	7.96	22.52	0.11	0.92	4.00
Greece	30.01	2.80	15.32	8.00	2.80	0.13	0.16	0.50
Ireland	48.19	5.41	35.73	6.48	—	0.14	—	—
Italy	33.61	11.19	42.59	6.18	11.13	0.12	—	0.77
Luxembourg	49.29	7.88	12.07	17.97	21.36	0.10	1.33	5.80
Netherlands	61.59	9.72	20.29	8.13	34.73	0.11	0.91	4.50
Portugal	22.07	16.99	21.67	3.87	8.36	0.12	0.35	1.86
Spain	21.84	20.86	24.41	3.08	7.49	0.11	0.34	1.75
Sweden	27.76	9.02	61.08	8.35	27.17	0.10	5.99	11.26
UK	61.97	14.04	46.73	5.55	60.85	0.14	3.45	4.54
EU15	34.91	12.68	32.72	5.88	27.75	0.13	1.44	3.20
Years								
1995–2015	X	X	X	X		X		
2008–15					X		X	X

Note: The table reports average crime rates (number of offences per 10,000 population) for different criminal offences in EU15 countries. The period covered by the data is indicated in the last two rows of the table.

Table A.11 *Property and drug crime and refugee population in EU15 countries – first differences estimates*

	(1)	(2)	(3)	(4)	(5)
Panel A: Property crime					
Burglary					
In (refugees/pop.)	−0.051**	−0.051**	−0.051**	−0.049**	−0.032
	(0.020)	(0.020)	(0.019)	(0.019)	(0.019)
Observations	312	312	294	291	274
Robbery					
In (refugees/pop.)	−0.068**	−0.068**	−0.051*	−0.051*	−0.037
	(0.031)	(0.030)	(0.027)	(0.028)	(0.025)
Observations	299	299	287	284	270
Vehicle theft					
In (refugees/pop.)	−0.004	−0.004	0.011	0.009	0.050
	(0.032)	(0.031)	(0.044)	(0.043)	(0.042)
Observations	316	316	300	298	281

Table A.11 (cont.)

	(1)	(2)	(3)	(4)	(5)
			Panel B: Drug crime		
In (refugees/pop.)	0.026	0.025	0.053	0.056	0.025
	(0.034)	(0.036)	(0.037)	(0.039)	(0.036)
Observations	300	300	288	285	272
Year dummies	Yes	Yes	Yes	Yes	Yes
Log (population)		Yes	Yes	Yes	Yes
Log GDP per capita			Yes	Yes	Yes
Youth employment rate				Yes	Yes
Share of pop. aged 15–24				Yes	Yes
Share of pop. with low education					Yes

Note: The table reports first differences estimates of changes in log property (panel A) and drug (panel B) crime rates on changes in the log of refugee population (per 10,000 residents). Period: 1995–2015. Sample: EU15 countries. Standard errors are clustered at the country level. $^{*}p < 0.1$; $^{**}p < 0.05$; $^{***}p < 0.01$.

Table A.12 *Property and drug crime and asylum applications in EU15 countries – first differences estimates*

	(1)	(2)	(3)	(4)	(5)
			Panel A: Property crime		
			Burglary		
In (refugees/pop.)	0.010	0.011	0.013	0.019	0.020
	(0.044)	(0.043)	(0.046)	(0.046)	(0.047)
Observations	202	202	202	202	198
			Robbery		
In (refugees/pop.)	−0.001	−0.000	0.000	0.002	0.004
	(0.031)	(0.031)	(0.031)	(0.031)	(0.031)
Observations	208	208	208	208	204
			Vehicle theft		
In (refugees/pop.)	0.031	0.032	0.035	0.039	0.050
	(0.038)	(0.036)	(0.040)	(0.040)	(0.042)
Observations	208	208	208	208	204

Table A.12 (cont.)

	(1)	(2)	(3)	(4)	(5)
			Panel B: Drug crime		
In (refugees/pop.)	0.031	0.028	0.029	0.034	0.014
	(0.037)	(0.037)	(0.038)	(0.039)	(0.040)
Observations	208	208	208	208	204
Year dummies	Yes	Yes	Yes	Yes	Yes
Log (population)		Yes	Yes	Yes	Yes
Log GDP per capita			Yes	Yes	Yes
Youth employment rate				Yes	Yes
Share of pop. aged 15–24				Yes	Yes
Share of pop. with low education					Yes

Note: The table reports first differences estimates of yearly changes in log property (panel A) and drug (panel B) crime rates on yearly changes in the log of asylum applications (per 10,000 residents). Period: 2000–2015. Sample: EU15 countries. Standard errors are clustered at the country level.

Table A.13 *Violent crime and refugee population in EU15 countries – first differences estimates*

	(1)	(2)	(3)	(4)	(5)
			Assault		
ln (asyl. appl./pop.)	−0.085	−0.093	−0.080	−0.086	−0.086
	(0.155)	(0.155)	(0.202)	(0.198)	(0.198)
Observations	105	105	105	105	105
			Homicide		
ln (asyl. appl./pop.)	0.019	0.019	0.041	0.045	0.102
	(0.034)	(0.035)	(0.073)	(0.074)	(0.104)
Observations	314	314	299	296	279
			Rape		
ln (asyl. appl./pop.)	−0.074	−0.077	−0.051	−0.059	−0.059
	(0.052)	(0.057)	(0.056)	(0.058)	(0.058)
Observations	98	98	98	98	98
			Sexual assault		
ln (asyl. appl./pop.)	−0.040	−0.047	−0.018	−0.013	−0.011
	(0.073)	(0.083)	(0.084)	(0.075)	(0.077)

Table A.13 (cont.)

	(1)	(2)	(3)	(4)	(5)
Observations	104	104	104	104	104
Year dummies	Yes	Yes	Yes	Yes	Yes
Log (population)		Yes	Yes	Yes	Yes
Log GDP per capita			Yes	Yes	Yes
Youth employment rate				Yes	Yes
Share of pop. aged 15–24				Yes	Yes
Share of pop. with low education					Yes

Note: The table reports first differences estimates of yearly changes in log violent crime rates on yearly changes in the log of refugee population (per 10,000 residents). Period: 1995–2015 for homicide and 2008–2014 for assault, rape, and sexual assault. Sample: EU15 countries. Standard errors are clustered at the country level.

Table A.14 *Violent crime and asylum applications in EU15 countries – first differences estimates*

	(1)	(2)	(3)	(4)	(5)
			Assault		
ln (asyl. appl./pop.)	-0.043	-0.042	-0.047	-0.066	-0.055
	(0.126)	(0.127)	(0.120)	(0.105)	(0.108)
Observations	96	96	96	96	96
			Homicide		
ln (asyl. appl./pop.)	0.038	0.039	0.039	0.048	0.043
	(0.085)	(0.084)	(0.083)	(0.084)	(0.087)
Observations	206	206	206	206	202
			Rape		
ln (asyl. appl./pop.)	-0.037	-0.035	-0.044	-0.060*	-0.060
	(0.041)	(0.042)	(0.038)	(0.032)	(0.034)
Observations	89	89	89	89	89
			Sexual assault		
ln (asyl. appl./pop.)	0.039	0.039	0.031	0.036	0.036
	(0.063)	(0.064)	(0.060)	(0.063)	(0.061)
Observations	95	95	95	95	95

Table A.14 (*cont.*)

	(1)	(2)	(3)	(4)	(5)
Year dummies	Yes	Yes	Yes	Yes	Yes
Log (population)		Yes	Yes	Yes	Yes
Log GDP per capita			Yes	Yes	Yes
Youth employment rate				Yes	Yes
Share of pop. aged 15–24				Yes	Yes
Share of pop. with low education					Yes

Note: The table reports first differences estimates of yearly changes in log violent crime rates on yearly changes in the log of asylum applications (per 10,000 residents). Period: 2000–2015 for homicide; 2008–14 for assault, rape, and sexual assault. Sample: EU15 countries. Standard errors are clustered at the country level. $^*p < 0.1$; $^{**}p < 0.05$; $^{***}p < 0.01$.

Table A.15 *Crime rates and refugee population: the timing of the effect – first differences estimates*

	(1)	(2)	(3)	(4)	(5)	(6)	(7)	(8)
	Panel A: Refugee population							
	Burglary		Robbery		Vehicle theft		Drug crime	
ln (refugees/pop.)	-0.027		-0.041		0.041		0.024	
	(0.017)		(0.025)		(0.034)		(0.034)	
First lag of ln (asyl. appl./pop.)	-0.035	-0.039	0.020	0.012	0.057	0.063	0.006	0.011
	(0.026)	(0.028)	(0.020)	(0.022)	(0.062)	(0.066)	(0.048)	(0.049)
Observations	274	274	270	270	281	281	272	272
	Plan B: Violent crime							
	Assault		Homicide		Rape		Sexual assault	
ln (refugees/pop.)	-0.107		0.107		-0.074		-0.032	
	(0.166)		(0.110)		(0.067)		(0.089)	
First lag of ln (asyl. appl./pop.)	0.073	0.037	-0.028	-0.012	0.056	0.032	0.067	0.055
	(0.156)	(0.183)	(0.087)	(0.082)	(0.069)	(0.071)	(0.103)	(0.097)
Observations	105	105	279	279	98	98	104	104
Year dummies	Yes	Yes	Yes	Yes	Yes	Yes	Yes	Yes
Other controls	Yes	Yes	Yes	Yes	Yes	Yes	Yes	Yes

Note: The table reports first differences estimates of yearly changes in log property and drug crime rates (panel A) and violent crime rates (panel B) on yearly changes in the log of refugee population (per 10,000 residents). 'Other controls' are log population, log GDP per capita, youth unemployment rate, share of population aged 15–24, share of population with low education. Period: 1995–2015 for property crime, drug crime, and homicide; 2008–14 for assault, rape, and sexual assault. Sample: EU15 countries. Standard errors are clustered at the country level.

Table A.16 *Crime rates and asylum applications: the timing of the effect – first differences estimates*

	(1)	(2)	(3)	(4)	(5)	(6)	(7)	(8)
	Panel A: Refugee population							
	Burglary		Robbery		Vehicle theft		Drug crime	
ln (refugees/pop.)	0.018		-0.001		0.040		0.007	
	(0.046)		(0.031)		(0.041)		(0.040)	
First lag of ln (asyl. appl./pop.)	-0.025	-0.026	0.003	0.003	-0.005	-0.011	0.015	0.014
	(0.050)	(0.052)	(0.033)	(0.034)	(0.032)	(0.029)	(0.034)	(0.037)
Observations	183	185	188	191	188	191	188	191
	Panel B: Violent crime							
	Assault		Homicide		Rape		Sexual assault	
ln (refugees/pop.)	-0.058		0.057		-0.063*		0.038	
	(0.099)		(0.097)		(0.034)		(0.061)	
First lag of ln (asyl. appl./pop.)	-0.074	-0.065	-0.031	-0.039	0.026	-0.003	0.046	0.048
	(0.186)	(0.181)	(0.106)	(0.100)	(0.059)	(0.005)	(0.056)	(0.054)
Observations	95	96	186	189	88	89	94	95
Year dummies	Yes	Yes	Yes	Yes	Yes	Yes	Yes	Yes
Other controls	Yes	Yes	Yes	Yes	Yes	Yes	Yes	Yes

Note: The table reports first differences estimates of yearly changes in log property and drug crime rates (panel A) and violent crime rates (panel B) on yearly changes in the log of asylum applications (per 10,000 residents). 'Other controls' are log population, log GDP per capita, youth unemployment rate, share of population aged 15–24, share of population with low education. Period: 2000–2015 for property crime, drug crime, and homicide; 2008–14 for assault, rape, and sexual assault. Standard errors are clustered at the country level. $^*p < 0.1$; $^{**}p < 0.05$; $^{***}p < 0.01$.

Table A.17 *Crime rates, refugees, and asylum applications in NMS13 countries – first differences estimates*

	(1)	(2)	(3)	(4)	(5)	(6)	(7)	(8)
				Panel A: Refugee population				
	Burglary		**Robbery**		**Vehicle theft**		**Drug crime**	
ln (refugees/pop.)	-0.101**	-0.107***	-0.019	0.000	-0.022	0.002	0.148	0.078
	(0.021)	(0.028)	(0.021)	(0.029)	(0.024)	(0.051)	(0.108)	(0.076)
Observations	192	167	197	174	199	172	186	170
	Assault		**Homicide**		**Rape**		**Sexual assault**	
ln (refugees/pop.)	0.073	0.087	-0.052	-0.112	0.002	0.013	-0.009	-0.013
	(0.074)	(0.075)	(0.055)	(0.079)	(0.074)	(0.096)	(0.068)	(0.093)
Observations	86	86	193	170	87	87	72	72
				Plan B: Asylum applications				
	Burglary		**Robbery**		**Vehicle theft**		**Drug crime**	
ln (refugees/pop.)	0.026	0.025	-0.012	-0.016	0.002	0.013	-0.009	-0.013
	(0.025)	(0.023)	(0.023)	(0.025)	(0.036)	(0.033)	(0.035)	(0.039)
Observations	139	139	141	141	139	139	138	138
	Assault		**Homicide**		**Rape**		**Sexual assault**	
ln (refugees/pop.)	0.034	0.047	0.024	0.028	-0.027	-0.027	-0.049	-0.058
	(0.049)	(0.049)	(0.035)	(0.037)	(0.065)	(0.066)	(0.058)	(0.055)
Observations	70	70	139	139	71	71	56	56
Year dummies	Yes	Yes	Yes	Yes	Yes	Yes	Yes	Yes
Other controls	Yes	Yes	Yes	Yes	Yes	Yes	Yes	Yes

Note: The table reports first differences estimates of yearly changes in log property, drug, and violent crime rates on yearly changes in the log of refugee population (per 10,000 residents; panel A) and of asylum applications (per 10,000 residents; panel B). 'Other controls' are log population, log GDP per capita, youth unemployment rate, share of population aged 15–24, share of population with low education. Sample: NMS13 countries. Standard errors are clustered at the country level. $^{*} p < 0.1$; $^{**} p < 0.05$; $^{***} p < 0.01$.

References

Abramitzky, R., and Boustan, L. P. (2017). Immigration in American economic history. *Journal of Economic Literature*, 55(4): 1311–45.

Abrams, D., Bertrand, M., and Mullainathan, S. (2012). Do judges vary in their treatment of race? *Journal of Legal Studies*, 41(2): 347–83.

Aliverti, A. (2013). Immigration offences: Trends in legislation and criminal and civil enforcement – Briefing. The Migration Observatory, University of Oxford.

Alonso-Borrego, C., Garoupa, N., and Vázquez, P. (2012). Does immigration cause crime? Evidence from Spain. *American Law and Economics Review*, 14(1): 165–91.

Altonji, J. G., and Card, D. (1991). The effects of immigration on the labor market outcomes of less-skilled natives. In J. M. Aboud and R. B. Freeman (eds.), *Immigration, Trade and the Labor Market*. Chicago, IL: University of Chicago Press, pp. 201–34.

Ambrosini, M. (2011). *Quanta ipocrisia in un click day*. Retrieved from: www .lavoce.info

Amuedo-Dorantes, Catalina, Bansak, Cynthia, and Pozo, Susan. (2018). Refugee admissions and public safety: Are refugee settlement areas more prone to crime? IZA Discussion Papers 11612. Institute for the Study of Labor.

Baker, S. R. (2014). *Effects of immigrant legalization on crime: The 1986 Immigration Reform and Control Act*. Stanford Law and Economics Olin Working Paper No. 412. Stanford, CA: Stanford School of Law. Retrieved from: http://ssrn.com/abstract=1829368

(2015). Effects of immigrant legalization on crime. *American Economic Review, Papers & Proceedings*, 105(5): 210–13.

Bansak, C., and Raphael, S. (2001). Immigration reform and the earnings of Latino workers: Do employer sanctions cause discrimination? *Industrial and Labor Relations Review*, 54(2): 275–95.

Barbarino, A., and Mastrobuoni, G. (2014). The incapacitation effect of incarceration: Evidence from several Italian collective pardons. *American Economic Journal: Economic Policy*, 6(1): 1–37.

Bartel, A. P. (1989). Where do the new United States immigrants live? *Journal of Labor Economics*, 7(4): 371–91.

Becker, G. (1968). Crime and punishment: An economic approach. *Journal of Political Economy*, 76: 175–209.

Becker, Sascha O., and Ferrara, Andreas. (forthcoming). Consequences of forced migration: A survey of recent findings. *Labour Economics*.

Bell, B., and Machin, S. (2013). Immigrant enclaves and crime. *Journal of Regional Science*, 53(1): 118–41.

Bell, B., Machin, S., Fasani, F., and Machin, S. (2013). Crime and immigration: Evidence from large immigrant waves. *The Review of Economics and Statistics*, 95(4): 1278–90.

Bevelander, Pieter. (2016). Integrating refugees into labor markets. *IZA World of Labor*, 269. DOI:10.15185/izawol.269.

Bevelander, Pieter, and Pendakur, Ravi. (2014). The labour market integration of refugee and family reunion immigrants: A comparison of outcomes in Canada and Sweden. *Journal of Ethnic and Migration Studies*, 40(5): 689–709.

Bianchi, M., Buonanno, P., and Pinotti, P. (2012). Do immigrants cause crime? *Journal of the European Economic Association*, 10(6): 1318–47.

Blangiardo, G. (2008). *The centre sampling technique in surveys on foreign migrants. The balance of a multi-year experience.* UNECE & EUROSTAT Working Paper No. 12. Geneva, Switzerland: United Nations Statistical Commission (UNECE) and European Commission Statistical Office of the European Communities (EUROSTAT). Retrieved from: www.unece.org/filead min/DAM/stats/documents/ece/ces/ge.10/2008/wp.12.e.pdf

Blumstein, A., and Nakamura, K. (2009). Redemption in the presence of widespread criminal background checks. *Criminology*, 47(2): 327–59.

Bodenhorn, H., Moehling C., and Piehl A. M. (2010). Immigration: America's nineteenth-century law and order problem. In G. S. Epstein and I. N. Gang (eds.), *Migration and Culture.* Frontiers of Economics of Globalization Series. Bingley, UK: Emerald Publishers, pp. 295–323.

Boeri, T., and Brücker, H. (2005). Why are Europeans so tough on migrants? *Economic Policy, CEPR; CES; MSH*, 20(44): 629–703.

Borjas, G. J. (1995). The economic benefits from immigration. *Journal of Economic Perspectives*, 9(2): 3–22.

(2001). "Does immigration grease the wheels of the labor market?" *Brookings Papers on Economic Activity*, 1: 69–133.

(2003). The labor demand curve is downward sloping: Reexamining the impact of immigration on the labor market. *The Quarterly Journal of Economics*, 118(4): 1335–74.

Bratsberg, Bernt, Raaum, Oddbjorn, and Roed, Knut. (2017). Immigrant labor market integration across admission classes. IZA Discussion Paper No. 10513. Bonn, Germany: Institute of Labor Economics (IZA).

Bustamente, J. (1990). Measuring the flow of undocumented immigrants: Research findings from the Zapata Canyon Project. In F. Bean, B. Edmonston, and J. Passel (eds.), *Undocumented Migration to the United States: IRCA and the Experience of the 1980s*. Washington, DC: Urban Institute, pp. 211–26.

Butcher, K. F., and Piehl, A. (1998). Cross-city evidence on the relationship between immigration and crime. *Journal of Policy Analysis and Management*, 17(3): 457–93.

(2007). Why are immigrants' incarceration rates so low? Evidence on selective immigration, deterrence, and deportation. NBER Working Paper No. 13229. Cambridge, MA: National Bureau of Economic Research.

Cadena, Brian C., and Kovak, Brian K. (2016). Immigrants equilibrate local labor markets: Evidence from the Great Recession: Dataset. *American Economic Journal: Applied Economics*, 8(1): 257–90.

Card, D. (2001). Immigrant inflows, native outflows, and the local market impacts of higher immigration. *Journal of Labor Economics*, 19: 22–64.

Casarico, A., Facchini, G., and Frattini, T. (2012). *What drives immigration amnesties?* CESifo Working Paper No. 3981. Munich, Germany: Center for Economic Studies and Ifo Institute (CESifo). Retrieved from: www.cesifo-group.de/portal/page/portal/CD58733BCE3D254DE04400144FAFBA7C

Clark, K., Drinkwater, S., and Robinson, C. (2014). Migration, economic crisis and adjustment in the UK. IZA Discussion Paper No. 8410. Bonn, Germany: Institute of the Study of Labor (IZA).

Comino, Stefano, Mastrobuoni, G., and Nicolò, A. (2016). Silence of the innocents: Illegal immigrants' underreporting of crime and their victimization. IZA Discussion Papers 10306. Institute for the Study of Labor. Working paper.

Conservative Party. (2010). *Invitation to Join the Government of Britain: The Conservative Manifesto 2010*. Westminster: Conservative Research Department.

Cortes, Kalena E. (2004). Are refugees different from economic immigrants? Some empirical evidence on the heterogeneity of immigrant groups in the United States. *Review of Economics and Statistics*, 86(2): 465–80.

Couttenier, Mathieu, Preotu, Veronica, Rohner, Dominic, and Thoenig, Mathias. (2016). The violent legacy of victimization: Post-conflict evidence on asylum seekers, crimes and public policy in Switzerland. CEPR Discussion Papers 11079. London: Centre for Economic Policy Research.

Dagnelie, Olivier, Mayda, Anna Maria, and Maystadt, Jean-François. (2017). Labor market integration of refugees to the United States: Do entrepreneurs in the network help? U.S. Department of State Office of the Chief Economist Working Paper 2017–04.

Damm, Anna Piil, and Dustmann, Christian. (2014). Does growing up in a high crime neighborhood affect youth criminal behavior? *American Economic Review*, 104(6): 1806–32.

De la Rica, Sara, Glitz, Albrecht, and Ortega, Francesc. (2015). Immigration in Europe: Trends, policies and empirical evidence. In Barry R. Chiswick and Paul W. Miller (eds.), *Handbook of the Economics of International Migration*, Vol. 1B. Amsterdam: North–Holland, pp. 1303–62.

Del Boca, D., and Venturini, A. (2003). *Italian migration*. IZA Discussion Paper No. 938. Bonn, Germany: Institute for the Study of Labor (IZA). Retrieved from: http://ftp.iza.org/dp938.pdf

Deming, D. J. (2011). Better schools, less crime? *Quarterly Journal of Economics*, 126(4): 2063–115.

Devillanova, C., Fasani, F., and Frattini, T. (2018). Employment of undocumented immigrants and the prospect of legal status: Evidence from an amnesty program. *Industrial and Labor Relations Review*, 71(4): 853–81.

Devitt, Camilla. (2012). Labour Migration governance in Contemporary Europe. The UK Case. Fieri Working papers, LAB-MIG-GOV Project "Which labour migration governance for a more dynamic and inclusive Europe?" Retrieved from: http://labmiggov.fieri.it/wp-content/uploads/2012/04/UK-case-study-FINAL.pdf

Dinas, E., and van Spanje, J. (2011). Crime story: The role of crime and immigration in the anti-immigration vote. *Electoral Studies*, 30(4): 658–71.

Donato, Katharine, and Carter, Rebecca. (1999). Mexico and U.S. policy on illegal immigration: A fifty-year retrospective. In David Haines and Karen Rosenblum (eds.), *Illegal Immigration in America*. Westport, CT: Greenwood Press, pp. 112–29.

Donato, Katharine, and Massey, Douglas. (1993). Effect of the Immigration Reform and Control Act on the wages of Mexican migrants. *Social Science Quarterly*, 74(3): 523–41.

Donato, K. M., Durand, J., and Massey, D. S. (1992a). Changing conditions in the U.S. labor market: Effects of the Immigration Reform and Control Act of 1986. *Population Research and Policy Review*, 11(2): 93–115.

(1992b). Stemming the tide: Assessing the deterrent effects of the Immigration Reform and Control Act. *Demography*, 29(2): 139–57.

(1993). Effect of the Immigration Reform and Control Act on the wages of Mexican migrants. *Social Science Quarterly*, 74(3): 523–41.

Drinkwater, S., Eade, J., and Garapich, M. (2009). Poles apart? EU enlargement and the labour market outcomes of immigrants in the UK. *International Migration*, 47: 161–90.

Dustmann, C., and Glitz, A. (2011). Migration and education. In E. A. Hanushek, S. Machin, and L. Woessmann (eds.), *Handbook of the Economics of Education*, Vol. 4. Amsterdam: North–Holland, pp. 327–439.

Dustmann, C., Glitz, A., and Vogel, T. (2010). Employment, wages, and the economic cycle: Differences between immigrants and natives. *European Economic Review*, 54(1): 1–17.

Dustmann, C., Fasani, F., and Speciale, B. (2017). Illegal migration and consumption behavior of immigrant households. *Journal of European Economic Association*, 15(3): 654–91.

Dustmann, C., Frattini, T., and Preston, I. (2013). The effect of immigration along the distribution of wages. *Review of Economic Studies*, 80(1): 145–73.

Dustmann, C., Fasani, F., Frattini, T., Minale, L., and Schönberg, U. (2017). On the economics and politics of refugee migration. *Economic Policy*, 32(91): 497–550.

European Migration Network. (2015). Determining labour shortages and the need for labour migration from third countries in the EU.

Facchini, G., and Mayda, A. M. (2008). From individual attitudes towards migrants to migration policy outcomes: Theory and evidence. *Economic Policy*, 23(56): 651–713.

(2009). Does the welfare state affect individual attitudes toward immigrants? Evidence across countries. *The Review of Economics and Statistics*, 91(2): 295–314.

Farrington, D. P. (1986). Age and crime. *Crime and Justice*, 7: 189–250.

(1998). Individual differences and offending. In M. Tonry (ed.), *The Handbook of Crime and Punishment*. New York: Oxford University Press, pp. 241–68.

Fasani, F. (2010). The quest for "La Dolce Vita"? Undocumented migration in Italy. In A. Triandafyllidou (ed.), *Irregular Migration in Europe: Myths and Realities*. Surrey, UK: Ashgate, pp. 167–86.

(2013). Improving access to labour market information for migrants and employers – Italy. In M. V. Desiderio and A. Schuster (eds.), *Improving Access to Labour Market Information for Migrants and Employers*. Brussels: International Organization for Migration (IOM) and DG Employment, Social Affairs and Inclusion of the European Commission, pp. 87–126.

(2018). Immigrant crime and legal status: Evidence from repeated amnesty programs. *Journal of Economic Geography*, 18(4): 887–914.

Fasani, F., Frattini, Tommaso, and Minale, Luigi. (2017). The (struggle for) labour market integration of refugees: Evidence from European countries. CReAM Discussion Paper Series 1716.

Fernández-Huertas Moraga, Jesùs, and Hillel, Rapoport. (2015). Tradable refugee-admission quotas and EU asylum policy. *CESifo Economic Studies*, 61: 638–72.

Freedman, Matthew, Owens, Emily, and Bohn, Sarah. (2018). Immigration, employment opportunities, and criminal behavior. *American Economic Journal: Economic Policy*, 10(2): 117–51.

Garcia, J. R. (1980). *Operation Wetback: The Mass Deportation of Mexican Undocumented Workers in 1954*. Westport, CT: Greenwood Press.

Gehrsitz, Markus, and Ungerer, Martin. (2017). Jobs, crime, and votes: A short-run evaluation of the refugee crisis in Germany. IZA Discussion Paper No. 10494. Institute for the Study of Labor.

Gibbons, S. (2004). The costs of urban property crime. *Economic Journal, Royal Economic Society*, 114(499): F441–F463.

Gold, M. B. (2011). *Forbidden Citizens: Chinese Exclusion and the U.S. Congress: A Legislative History*. Alexandria, VA: TheCapitol.Net, Inc.

Goldin, C. (1994). The political economy of immigration restriction in the United States, 1890 to 1921. In C. Goldin and G. Libecap (eds.), *The Regulated Economy: A Historical Approach to Political Economy*. Chicago: University of Chicago Press, pp. 223–58.

Gordon, I., Scanlon, K., Travers, T., and Whitehead, C. (2009). *Economic Impact on the London and UK Economy of an Earned Regularisation of Irregular Migrants to the UK*. London, UK: Greater London Authority.

Hainmueller, J., Hangartner, D., and Lawrence, D. (2016). When lives are put on hold: Lengthy asylum processes decrease employment among refugees. *Science Advances*, 2(8). DOI:10.1126/sciadv.1600432.

Hale, C. (1996). Fear of crime: A review of the literature. *International Review of Victimology*, 4(2): 79–150.

Hatton, Timothy J. (2009). The rise and fall of asylum: What happened and why? *Economic Journal, Royal Economic Society*, 119(535): 183–213.

(2015). Asylum policy in the EU: The case for deeper integration. *CESifo Economic Studies*, 61: 605–37.

(2016). Refugees, asylum seekers, and policy in OECD countries.*American Economic Review*, 106(5): 441–45.

Hanson, G. H. (2009). *The Economics and Policy of Illegal Immigration in the United States*. Washington, DC: Migration Policy Institute.

Hanson, G. H., Scheve, K., and Slaughter, M. J. (2007). Public finance and individual preferences over globalization strategies, economics and politics. *Economics & Politics*, 19(1): 1–33.

Hatton, T. J. (2005). Explaining trends in UK immigration. *Journal of Population Economics*, 18(4): 719–40.

Hatton, T. J., and Williamson, J. G. (2005). *A dual policy paradox: Why have trade and immigration policies always differed in labor-scarce economies?* NBER Working Paper No. 11866. Cambridge, MA: National Bureau of Economic Research. Retrieved from: http://dx.doi.org/10.3386/w11866

Higham, J. (1955). *Strangers in the Land: Patterns of American Nativism, 1860–1925.* Westport, CT: Greenwood Press.

Hjalmarsson, R., Holmlund, H., and Lindquist, M. J. (2015). The effect of education on criminal convictions and incarceration: Causal evidence from micro-data. *Economic Journal*, 125(587): 1290–326.

Hoefer, M., Rytina, N., and Baker, B. (1991). Background of US immigration policy reform. In F. L. Rivera-Batiz, S. Sechzer, and I. Gang (eds.), *US Immigration Policy Reform in the 1980s: A Preliminary Assessment.* New York: Praeger, pp. 17–44.

(2009). *Estimates of the unauthorized immigrant population residing in the United States: January 2008.* Washington, DC: US Department of Homeland Security. Retrieved from: www.dhs.gov/xlibrary/assets/statistics/publications/ois_ill_pe_2008.pdf

Home Office. (2016a). Immigration statistics, January to March 2016.

(2016b). Crime in England and Wales: Year ending March 2016.

Italian Ministry of Interior. (2007). Rapporto sulla criminalità in Italia. Analisi, Prevenzione, Contrasto.

Jaitman, L., and Machin, S. (2013). Crime and immigration: New evidence from England and Wales. *IZA Journal of Migration*, 2(1): 1–23.

Kerr, S. P., and Kerr, W. R. (2011). *Economic impacts of immigration: A survey.* NBER Working Paper No. 16736. Cambridge, MA: National Bureau of Economic Research. Retrieved from: http://dx.doi.org/10.3386/w16736

Kossoudji, S., and Cobb-Clark, D. (2002). Coming out of the shadows: Learning about legal status and wages from the legalized population. *Journal of Labor Economics*, 20(3): 598–628.

Lee, D. S. (2008). Randomized experiments from non-random selection in US House elections. *Journal of Econometrics*, 142(2): 675–97.

Lee, D. S., and Lemieux, T. (2010). Regression discontinuity designs in economics. *Journal of Economic Literature*, 48: 281–355.

Lochner, L., and Moretti, E. (2004). The effect of education on crime: Evidence from prison inmates, arrests, and self-reports. *American Economic Review*, 94: 155–80.

Machin, S., Marie, O., and Vujic, S. (2011). The crime reducing effect of education. *Economic Journal*, 121: 463–84.

Marbach, M., Hainmueller, J., and Hangartner, D. (2018). The long-term impact of employment bans on the economic integration of refugees. *Science Advances*, 4(9). DOI:10.1126/sciadv.aap9519.

Martin, P. (2003). *Promise Unfulfilled: Unions, Immigration, and Farm Workers*. Ithaca, NY: Cornell University Press.

Massey, Douglas. (1987). Do undocumented migrants earn lower wages than legal immigrants? New evidence from Mexico. *International Migration Review*, 21: 236–74.

Mastrobuoni, G., and Pinotti, P. (2015). Legal status and the criminal activity of immigrants. *American Economic Journal: Applied Economics*, 7(2): 175–206.

Mayda, A. M. (2006). Who is against immigration? A cross-country investigation of individual attitudes toward immigrants. *The Review of Economics and Statistics*, 88(3): 510–30.

(2008). Why are people more pro-trade than pro-migration? *Economics Letters*, 101(3): 160–63.

Meyers, E. (2004). *International Immigration Policy: A Theoretical and Comparative Analysis*. Houndmills, UK: Palgrave Macmillan.

Moehling, C. M., and Piehl, A. M. (2009). Immigration, crime, and incarceration in early 20th century America. *Demography*, 46: 739–763.

(2014). Immigrant assimilation into U.S. prisons, 1900–1930. *Journal of Population Economics*, 27: 173–200.

Moffitt, T., Ross, S., and Raine, A. (2011). Crime and biology. In J. Wilson and J. Petersilia (eds.), *Crime and Public Policy*. New York: Oxford University Press, pp. 53–87.

Mustard, D. B. (2001). Racial, ethnic, and gender disparities in sentencing: Evidence from the US federal courts. *Journal of Law and Economics*, 44 (1): 285–314.

National Audit Office. (2014). Managing and removing foreign national offenders. Report by the Comptroller and Auditor General.

Ngai, M. (2004). *Impossible Subjects: Illegal Aliens and the Making of Modern America*. Princeton, NJ: Princeton University Press.

Nunziata, L. (2015). Immigration and crime: Evidence from victimization data. *Journal of Population Economics*, 28(3): 697–736.

Orrenius, P. M., and Zavodny, M. (2003). Do amnesty programs reduce undocumented immigration? Evidence from IRCA. *Demography*, 40(3): 437–50.

Ortega, F., and Polavieja, J. G. (2012). Labor-market exposure as a determinant of attitudes toward immigration. *Labour Economics*, 19: 298–311.

Ottaviano, G., and Peri, G. (2006). The economic value of cultural diversity: Evidence from US cities. *Journal of Economic Geography*, 6: 9–44.

(2012). Rethinking the effect of immigration on wages. *Journal of the European Economic Association*, 10(1): 152–197.

Ousey, G. C., and Kubrin, C. E. (2018). Immigration and crime: Assessing a contentious issue. *Annual Review of Criminology*, 1: 63–84.

Pager, D. (2003). The mark of a criminal record. *American Journal of Sociology*, 108 (5): 937–75.

Passel, J., and Cohn, D. (2008). *Trends in Unauthorized Immigration: Undocumented Inflow Now Trails Legal Inflow*. Washington, DC: Pew Hispanic Center.

Pinkerton, C., McLaughlan, G., and Salt, J. (2004). *Sizing the Illegally Resident Population in the UK*. London, UK: Home Office.

Pinotti, P. (2017). Clicking on heaven's door: The effect of immigrant legalization on crime. *American Economic Review*, 107(1): 138–68.

Pleasants, J. (2000). *Buncombe Bob: The Life and Times of Robert Rice Reynolds*. Chapel Hill, NC: University of North Carolina Press.

Pope, J. C. (2008). Fear of crime and housing prices: Household reactions to sex offender registries. *Journal of Urban Economics*, 64(3): 601–14.

Porter, Matthew, and Haslam, Nick. (2005). Predisplacement and postdisplacement factors associated with mental health of refugees and internally displaced persons: A meta–analysis. *JAMA*, 294(5): 602–12.

Reid, L. W., Weiss, H. E., Adelman, R. M., and Jaret, C. (2005). The immigration–crime relationship: Evidence across US metropolitan areas. *Social Science Research*, 34(4): 757–80.

Reyneri, E. (2003). Immigration and the underground economy in new receiving South European countries: Manifold negative effects, manifold deep-rooted causes. *International Review of Sociology*, 13(1): 117–43.

Rivera-Batiz, F. (1999). Undocumented workers in the labor market: An analysis of the earnings of legal and illegal immigrants in the United States. *Journal of Population Economics*, 12(1): 91–116.

Rytina, N. (2002). *IRCA Legalization Effects: Lawful Permanent Residence and Naturalization through 2001*. Washington, DC: Office of Policy and Planning Statistics Division U.S. Immigration and Naturalization Service. Retrieved from: http://uscis.gov/graphics/shared/aboutus/statistics/IRCA_REPORT/irc a0114int.pdf

Sampson, R. J. (2008). Rethinking crime and immigration. *Contexts*, 7(1): 28–33.

Scheve, K. F., and Slaughter, M. J. (2001). Labor-market competition and individual preferences over immigration policy. *Review of Economics and Statistics*, 83 (1): 133–45.

Shihadeh, E. S., and Barranco, R. E. (2010). Latino employment and Black violence: The unintended consequence of US immigration policy. *Social Forces*, 88(3): 1393–420.

(2013). The imperative of place: Homicide and the new Latino migration. *The Sociological Quarterly*, 54(1): 81–104.

Spann, G. (2004). The darker side of Grutter. *Constitutional Commentary*, 21: 221–50.

Staiger, D., and Stock, J. H. (1997) Instrumental variables regression with weak instruments. *Econometrica*, 65(3): 557–86.

Storesletten, K. (2000). Sustaining fiscal policy through immigration. *Journal of Political Economy*, 108(2): 300–23.

Thistlethwaite, D. L., and Campbell, D. T. (1960). Regression-discontinuity analysis: An alternative to the ex post facto experiment. *Journal of Educational Psychology*, 51(6): 309–17.

Transatlantic Trends. (2011). *Transatlantic trends: Immigration, key findings 2011*. Retrieved from: http://trends.gmfus.org/immigration/about/

UK Ministry of Justice. (2016). *Guide to offender management statistics – England and Wales*. Guidance documentation. Retrieved from: www.gov.uk/govern ment/uploads/system/uploads/attachment_data/file/541251/guide.pdf

UNHCR. (2014). UNHCR global trends 2013: War's human cost. UN High Commissioner for Refugees.

Wadsworth, T. (2010). Is immigration responsible for the crime drop? An assessment of the influence of immigration on changes in violent crime between 1990 and 2000. *Social Science Quarterly*, 91(2): 531–53.

Wang, X. (1997). *The Trial of Democracy: Black Suffrage and Northern Republicans, 1860–1910*. Athens, GA: University of Georgia Press.

Woodrow, K. A., and Passel, J. S. (1990). Post-IRCA undocumented immigration to the United States: An assessment based on the June 1988 CPS. In F. Bean, B. Edmonston, and J. Passel (eds.), *Undocumented Migration to the United States—IRCA and the Experience of the 1980s*. Washington, DC: Urban Institute, pp. 33–76.

Index